Advance Praise for

PEAK EVERYTHING

Richard Heinberg brings important news that few will want to hear
— the limits we've been hearing about for four decades are really
upon us. He also brings a pretty good hint of the directions we
might take to escape the tightening knot. An important book from
an important thinker.

— Bill McKibben, author *Deep Economy:*
the Wealth of Communities and the Durable Future

There are few harder questions than the ones Richard Heinberg
takes on in *Peak Everything*. Fortunately, he addresses them with his
customary fearlessness, intellectual rigor and good sense. More
than anyone else I've encountered, Heinberg has an answer to the
most fundamental question of all; "How shall we go on from here."
Reading this, I can believe there is hope that we can.

— Sharon Astyk, farmer,
publisher of Cansabon's Book blog,
author of *The New Home Front:*
Families and the Coming Ecological Crisis (in press)

Once again — and with eyes as peeled to the task as a Buddha's —
Richard Heinberg jumps into the cauldron of global resource decline. This is his most integrated report from the social, economic,
and ecological contraction now unfolding, which he delivers with
mindfulness, compassion, and a view to humanity's strengths.

— Chellis Glendinning,
author of *My Name Is Chellis and I'm in*
Recovery from Western Civilization

Peak Oil is a great threat to our way of life, and Richard Heinberg is
one of the world's best-known writers and analysts of the subject. In
Peak Everything, Heinberg gives us a series of provocative essays
about the profound individual and global implications of Peak Oil.

— Albert A. Bartlett, Professor Emeritus of Physics,
University of Colorado at Boulder

PEAK EVERYTHING

PEAK EVERYTHING

WAKING UP to the CENTURY OF DECLINES

RICHARD HEINBERG

NEW SOCIETY PUBLISHERS

CATALOGING IN PUBLICATION DATA

A catalog record for this publication is available
from the National Library of Canada.

Cover design and illustration by Diane McIntosh.

Printed in Canada.
First printing July 2007.

Hardcover ISBN: 978-0-86571-598-1

Inquiries regarding requests to reprint all or part of *Peak Everything*
should be addressed to New Society Publishers at the address below.
To order directly from the publishers, please call toll-free
(North America) 1-800-567-6772, or order online at
www.newsociety.com

Any other inquiries can be directed by mail to:
New Society Publishers
P.O. Box 189, Gabriola Island, BC V0R 1X0, Canada
(250) 247-9737

New Society Publishers' mission is to publish books that contribute in
fundamental ways to building an ecologically sustainable and just society,
and to do so with the least possible impact on the environment, in a manner
that models this vision. We are committed to doing this not just through
education, but through action. This book is one step toward ending global
deforestation and climate change. It is printed on acid-free paper that is
100% post-consumer recycled (100% old growth forest-free), processed
chlorine free, and printed with vegetable-based, low-VOC inks, with covers
produced using Forest Stewardship Council-certified stock. Additionally,
New Society purchases carbon offsets annually, operating with a carbon-
neutral footprint. For further information, or to browse our full list of
books and purchase securely, visit our website at: www.newsociety.com

NEW SOCIETY PUBLISHERS   www.newsociety.com

Contents

Introduction: Peak Everything 1

ON TECHNOLOGY, AGRICULTURE, AND THE ARTS

1. Tools with a Life of Their Own 31
2. Fifty Million Farmers 47
3. (*post-*) Hydrocarbon Aesthetics 67

ON NATURE'S LIMITS AND THE HUMAN CONDITION

4. Five Axioms of Sustainability 85
5. Parrots and Peoples 97
6. Population, Resources, and Human Idealism 113

THE END OF ONE ERA, THE BEGINNING OF ANOTHER

7. The Psychology of Peak Oil and Climate Change 127
8. Bridging Peak Oil and Climate Change Activism 141
9. Boomers' Last Chance? 159
10. A Letter From the Future 173
11. Talking Ourselves to Extinction 185

Resources for Action 199
Notes 201
Index 207
About the Author 213

Acknowledgments

It would be impossible to thank everyone who has helped with this book in some way. The chapters herein developed over many months, during which I was traveling a great deal and speaking to audiences large and small about the problem of oil depletion, its likely consequences, and what we can do to wean our societies from our collective addiction to fossil fuels. I met hundreds of people during these travels whose words and pioneering actions are reflected in these pages.

Once again, I must acknowledge an enormous debt of gratitude to my wife Janet Barocco, who supports and balances me in so many ways as I pursue the rather lopsided life of a writer-lecturer.

This is the fourth book project on which I have had the pleasure of working with Chris and Judith Plant of New Society Publishers. A note of appreciation must also go to Ingrid Witvoet, who shepherded the book through the production process, and Murray Reiss, who copy-edited the manuscript.

My thanks to Jennifer Bresee for research assistance, and to Susan Williamson for general assistance.

As in the past, my students and co-faculty at New College deserve mention for their ongoing support, as do the subscribers to my monthly *MuseLetter*.

Finally, I would like to voice both appreciation and thanks to Julian Darley and Celine Rich-Darley — founders of Post Carbon Institute, and catalysts in the global response to the twin crises of fossil fuels (climate change and resource depletion).

Introduction: Peak Everything

D URING THE PAST few years the phrase *Peak Oil* has entered
the global lexicon. It refers to that moment in time when the
world will achieve its maximum possible rate of oil extraction; from
then on, for reasons having mostly to do with geology, the amount
of petroleum available to society on a daily or yearly basis will begin
to dwindle. Most informed analysts agree that this will happen during the next two or three decades; an increasing number believe
that it is happening now — that conventional oil production peaked
in 2005–2006 and that the flow to market of all hydrocarbon liquids taken together will start to diminish around 2010.[1] The consequences, as they begin to accumulate, are likely to be severe: the
world is overwhelmingly dependent on oil for transportation,
agriculture, plastics, and chemicals; thus a lengthy process of adjustment will be required. According to one recent US government-
sponsored study, if the peak does occur soon replacements are
unlikely to appear quickly enough and in sufficient quantity to avert
what it calls "unprecedented" social, political, and economic impacts.[2]

This book is not an introduction to the subject of Peak Oil; several existing volumes serve that function (including my own *The
Party's Over: Oil, War and the Fate of Industrial Societies*).[3] Instead

it addresses the social and historical context in which Peak Oil is occurring, and explores how we can reorganize our thinking and action in several critical areas to better navigate this perilous time.

Our socio-historical context takes some time and perspective to appreciate. Upon first encountering Peak Oil, most people tend to assume it is merely a single isolated problem to which there is a simple solution — whether of an eco-friendly nature (more renewable energy) or otherwise (more coal). But prolonged reflection and study tend to eat away at the viability of such "solutions." Meanwhile, as one contemplates how we humans have so quickly become so deeply dependent on the cheap, concentrated energy of oil and other fossil fuels, it is difficult to avoid the conclusion that we have caught ourselves on the horns of the Universal Ecological Dilemma, consisting of the interlinked elements of population pressure, resource depletion, and habitat destruction — on a scale unprecedented in history.

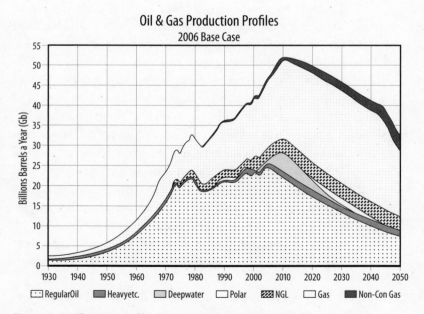

Figure 1. Production profiles for world oil and natural gas, history and forecast. Credit: Association for the Study of Peak Oil and Gas (ASPO)

Petroleum is not the only important resource quickly depleting. Readers already acquainted with the Peak Oil literature know that regional production peaks for natural gas have already occurred, and that over the short term the economic consequences of gas shortages are likely to be even worse for Europeans and North Americans than those for oil. And while coal is often referred to as being an abundant fossil fuel, with reserves capable of supplying the world at current rates of usage for two hundred years into the future, recent studies updating global reserves and production forecasts conclude that global coal production will peak and begin to decline in ten to twenty years.[4] Because fossil fuels supply about 85 percent of the world's total energy, peaks in these fuels virtually ensure that the world's energy supply will begin to shrink within a few

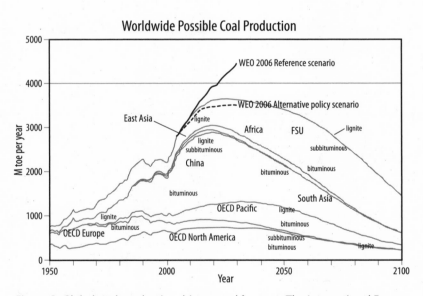

Figure 2. Global coal production, history and forecast. The International Energy Agency's "World Energy Outlook 2006" (WEO 2006) discusses two future scenarios for global coal production: a "reference scenario" that assumes unconstrained coal consumption, and an "alternative policy scenario" in which consumption is capped through government efforts to reduce climate impacts. Both scenarios are compatible with the supply forecast here (EWG report, 2007) until about 2020. Thereafter, only a rate of demand corresponding with the "alternative policy scenario" can be met. Credit: Energy Watch Group (EWG)

years regardless of any efforts that are made to develop other energy sources.

Nor does the matter end with natural gas and coal. Once one lifts one's eyes from the narrow path of daily survival activities and starts scanning the horizon, a frightening array of peaks comes into view. In the course of the present century we will see an end to growth and a commencement of decline in all of these parameters:

- Population
- Grain production (total and per capita)
- Uranium production
- Climate stability
- Fresh water availability per capita
- Arable land in agricultural production
- Wild fish harvests
- Yearly extraction of some metals and minerals (including copper, platinum, silver, gold, and zinc)

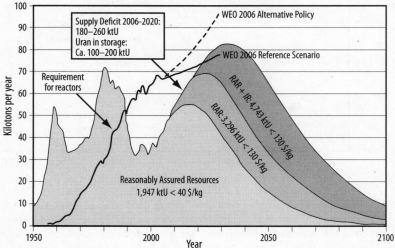

Figure 3. Global uranium supply from known resources, history and forecast, compared with supply requirements. Credit: EWG 2006, data from International Energy Agency (IEA) 2006

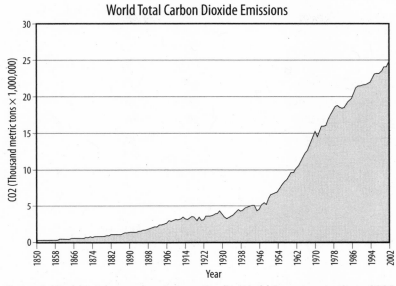

Figure 4. World total annual emissions. Credit: World Resources Institute 2005

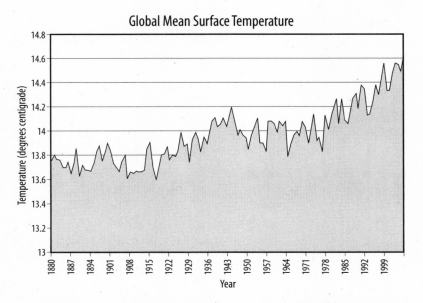

Figure 5. Global mean surface temperature. Credit: World Resources Institute 2005

The point of this book is not to go systematically through these peak-and-decline scenarios one by one, offering evidence and pointing out the consequences — though that is a worthwhile exercise, and it is instructive to contemplate a few graphs showing the general trends (see figures 1 through 5). Some of these peaks are more speculative than others. Fish harvests are already in decline, so this one is hardly arguable; however, projecting extraction peaks and declines for some metals requires extrapolating current rising rates of usage many decades into the future.[5] The problem of uranium supply beyond mid-century is well attested by studies, but has not received sufficient public attention.[6]

Nevertheless, the general picture is inescapable: it is one of mutually interacting instances of overconsumption and emerging scarcity.

Our starting point, then, is the realization that we are today living at the end of the period of greatest material abundance in human history — an abundance based on temporary sources of

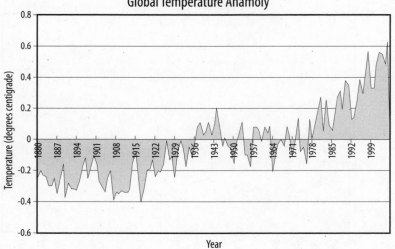

Figure 6. The global temperature anomaly is a measure of the difference between the mean global temperature at a given point in time and the average global temperature during the 20th century. Credit: Goddard Institute for Space Studies

cheap energy that made all else possible. Now that the most important of those sources are entering their inevitable sunset phase, we
are at the beginning of a period of overall societal contraction.

This realization is strengthened as we come to understand that it
is no happenstance that so many peaks are occurring together. They
are all causally related by the historic reality that, for the past 200
years, cheap, abundant energy from fossil fuels has driven technological invention, increases in total and per-capita resource extraction and consumption (including food production), and population
growth. We are enmeshed in a classic self-reinforcing feedback loop:

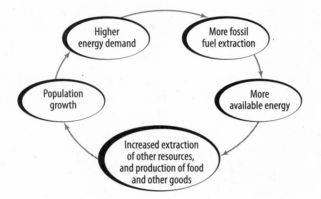

Self-reinforcing feedback loops sometimes occur in nature
(population blooms are always evidence of some sort of reinforcing
feedback loop), but they rarely continue for long. They usually lead
to population crashes and die-offs. The simple fact is that growth in
population and consumption cannot continue unabated on a finite
planet.

If the increased availability of cheap energy has historically enabled unprecedented growth in the extraction rates of other resources, then the coincidence of Peak Oil with the peaking and
decline of many other resources is entirely predictable.

Moreover, as the availability of energy resources peaks, this will
also affect various parameters of social welfare:

• Per-capita consumption levels

- Economic growth
- Easy, cheap, quick mobility
- Technological change and invention
- Political stability

All of these are clearly related to the availability of energy and other critical resources. Once we accept that energy, fresh water, and food will become less freely available over the next few decades, it is hard to escape the conclusion that while the 20th century saw the greatest and most rapid expansion of the scale, scope, and complexity of human societies in history, the 21st will see contraction and simplification. The only real question is whether societies will contract and simplify intelligently or in an uncontrolled, chaotic fashion.

Good News? Bad News?

None of this is easy to contemplate. Nor can this information easily be discussed in polite company: the suggestion that we are at or near the peak of population and consumption levels for the entirety of human history, and that it's all downhill from here, is not likely to win votes, lead to a better job, or even make for pleasant dinner banter. Most people turn off and tune out when the conversation moves in this direction; advertisers and news organizations take note and act accordingly. The result: a general, societal pattern of denial.

Where might we find solace in all this gloom? Well, it could be argued that some not-so-good things will also peak this century:

- Economic inequality
- Environmental destruction
- Greenhouse gas emissions

Why economic inequality? The late, great social philosopher Ivan Illich argued in his 1974 book *Energy and Equity* that inequality increases along with the flow of energy through a society. "[O]nly a ceiling on energy use," he wrote, "can lead to social relations that are characterized by high levels of equity."[7] Hunters and gatherers, who survived on minimal energy flows, also lived in societies nearly free from economic inequality. While some forager societies were

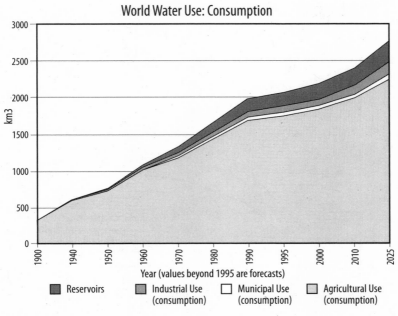

Figure 7. World water use, consumption. Credit: UNESCO

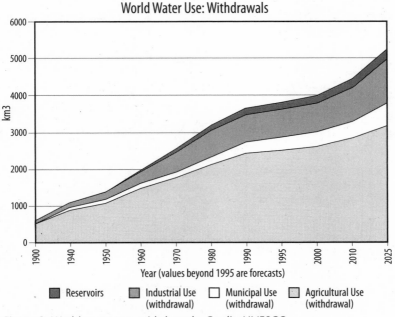

Figure 8. World water use, withdrawals. Credit: UNESCO

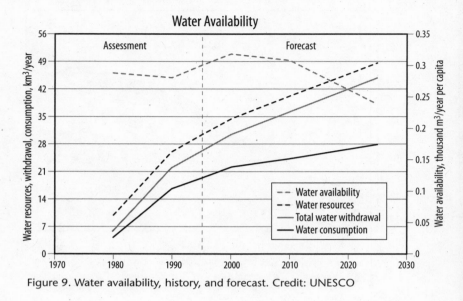

Figure 9. Water availability, history, and forecast. Credit: UNESCO

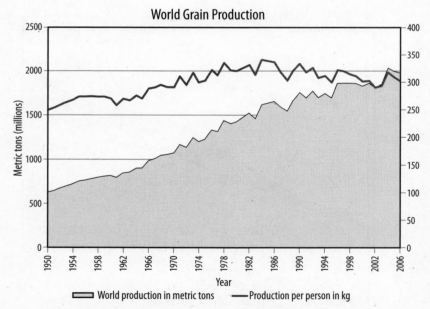

Figure 10. Annual world grain production, total amounts and amounts per capita. Credit: Earth Policy Institute

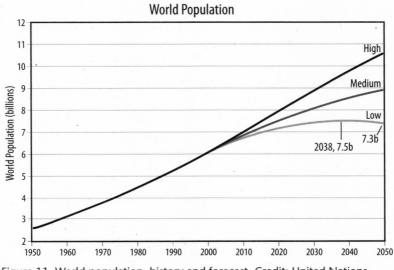

Figure 11. World population, history and forecast. Credit: United Nations Population Division, World Population Prospects

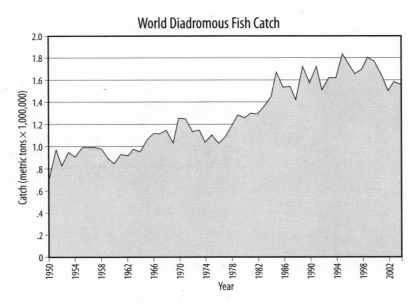

Figure 12. Annual marine (saltwater) fish catch. Credit: Food and Agriculture Organization © Luca Garibaldi

better off than others because they lived in more abundant ecosystems, the members of any given group tended to share equally whatever was available. Theirs was a gift economy — as opposed to the barter, market, and money economies that we are more familiar with. With agriculture and full-time division of labor came higher energy flow rates as well as widening economic disparity between kings, their retainers, and the peasant class. In the 20th century, with per capita energy flow rates soaring far above any in history, some humans enjoyed unprecedented material abundance, such that they expected that poverty could be eliminated once and for all if only the political will could be summoned. Indeed, during the

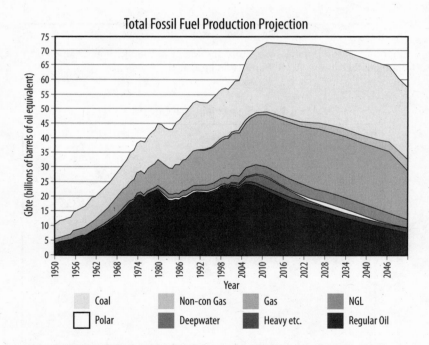

Figure 13. Combined oil, gas, and coal production projections, in billions of barrels of oil equivalent per year. This graph shows the probable future for fossils fuels, the source of roughly 85 percent of the world's current energy budget. Credit: Joe Atkinson, Powerswitch UK; data for oil and gas from the Association for the Study of Peak Oil and Gas (ASPO); data for coal from Energy Watch Group (EWG).

middle years of the century progress was seemingly being made along those lines. However, for the century in total, inequality actually increased. The Gini index, invented in 1912 as a measure of economic inequality within societies, has risen substantially within many nations (including the US, Britain, India, and China) in the past three decades, and economic disparity between rich and poor nations has also grown.[8] In the decades just prior to the 20th century, the average income in the world's wealthiest country was about ten times more than that in the poorest; now it is over forty-five times more. According to one study released in December, 2006 ("The World Distribution of Household Wealth,") the richest one percent of people now controls 40 percent of the world's wealth, while the richest two percent control fully half.[9] If this correlation between energy flow rates and inequality holds, it seems likely that, as available energy decreases during the 21st century, we are likely to see a reversion to lower levels of inequality. This is not to say that by century's end we will all be living in an egalitarian

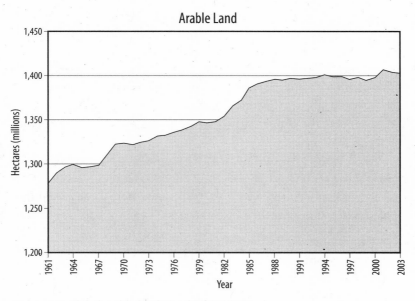

Figure 14. Global arable land. Credit: FAO 2006

socialist paradise, merely that the levels of inequality we see today will have become unsupportable.

Similarly, it seems likely that levels of humanly generated environmental destruction will peak and begin to recede in decades to come. As available energy declines, our ability to alter the environment will do so as well. However, if we make no deliberate attempt to control our impact on the biosphere, the peak will be a very high one and we will do an immense amount of damage along the way. On the other hand, we could expend deliberate and intelligent effort to reduce environmental impacts, in which case the peak will be at a lower level. Especially in the former case, this peak is likely to lag behind the others discussed, because many environmental harms involve reinforcing feedback loops as well as delayed and cumulative impacts that will continue to reverberate for decades after human population and consumption levels start to diminish. As the primary example of this, annual greenhouse gas emissions will undoubtedly peak in this century — whether as a result of voluntary reductions in fossil fuel consumption, or depletion of the resource base, or societal collapse. However, the global climate may not stabilize until many decades thereafter, until various reinforcing feedback loops that have been set in motion (such as the melting of the north polar icecap, which would expose dark water that would in turn absorb more heat, thus exacerbating the warming effect; and the melting of tundra and permafrost, releasing stored methane that would likewise greatly exacerbate warming) play themselves out. Indeed, the climate may not return to a phase of relative equilibrium for centuries.

Well, if the goal of the last few paragraphs was to balance bad-news peaks with cheerier ones, that effort so far seems less than entirely successful. Surely we can do better. Are there some *good* things that are *not* at or near their historic peaks? I can think of a few:

- Community
- Personal autonomy
- Satisfaction from honest work well done
- Intergenerational solidarity

- Cooperation
- Leisure time
- Happiness
- Ingenuity
- Artistry
- Beauty of the built environment

Of course, some of these items are hard to quantify. But a few can indeed be measured, and efforts to do so often yield surprising results. Let's consider two that have been subjects of quantitative study.

Leisure time is perhaps the element on this list that lends itself most readily to measurement. The most leisurely societies were without doubt those of hunter-gatherers, who worked about 1,000 hours per year, though these societies seldom if ever thought of dividing "work time" from "leisure time," since all activities were considered pleasurable in their way.[10] For US employees, hours worked peaked in the early industrial period, around 1850, at about 3,500 hours per year.[11] This was up from 1,620 hours worked annually by the typical medieval peasant. However, the two situations are not directly comparable: a typical medieval workday stretched from dawn to dusk (16 hours in summer, 8 in winter), but work was intermittent, with breaks for breakfast, midmorning refreshment, lunch, a customary afternoon nap, mid-afternoon refreshment, and dinner; moreover, there were dozens of holidays and festivals scattered throughout the year. Today the average US worker spends about 2,000 hours on the job each year, a figure somewhat higher than it was a couple of decades ago (in 1985 it was closer to 1,850 hours). Nevertheless, an historical overview suggests that the time-intensiveness of human labor seems to peak in the early phase of industrialization, and that a simplification of the modern economy could result in a reversion to older, pre-industrial norms.

In recent years the field of happiness research has flourished, with the publication of scores of studies and several books devoted to statistical analysis of what gives people a sense of overall satisfaction with their lives. International studies of self-reported levels of happiness show that once basic survival needs are met, there is little correlation between happiness and per capita consumption of fossil fuels. According to surveys, people in Mexico, who use fossil fuels at one-fifth the rate of US citizens, are just as happy. (See Figure 15.)

The opportunities to continue to enjoy current (or even higher) levels of happiness and to reduce work hours may seem pale comforts in light of all the enormous social and economic challenges implicit in the peaks discussed earlier. However, it is worth remembering that the list above details things that matter very much to most people in terms of their real, lived experience. The sense of community and the experience of intergenerational solidarity are literally priceless, in that no amount of money can buy them; moreover, life without them is bleak indeed — especially during times of social stress. And there are many reasons to think that these two factors have declined significantly during the past few decades of rapid urbanization and economic growth.

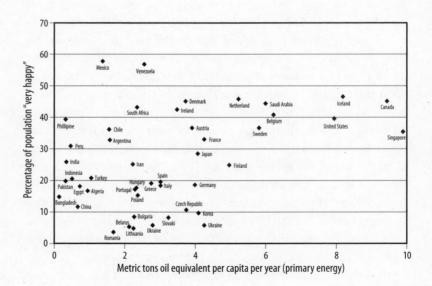

Figure 15. How self-reported levels of happiness vary according to per-capita annual energy consumption in various nations. Credit: Data from BP, World Values Survey, and the UN, put in graphic form by Nathan John Hagens.

In contrast with these indices of personal and social well-being, Gross Domestic Product (GDP) per capita is easily measured and shows a mostly upward trend for the world as a whole over the past two centuries. But it takes into account only a narrow set of data — the market value of all final goods and services produced within a country in a given period of time. Growth in GDP is used to tell us that we should be feeling better about ourselves and our world — but it leaves out a wide range of other factors, including damage to the environment, wars, crime and imprisonment rates, and trends in education (like whether more or fewer people graduate from high school or college, and the quality of the education received.) Many economists and non-governmental organizations have criticized governmental reliance on GDP for this reason, and have instead promoted the use of a Genuine Progress Indicator (GPI), which does take account of such factors. While a historical GDP chart for the US shows general ongoing growth up to the present (GDP correlates closely with energy consumption), GPI calculations show a peak around 1980 followed by a slow decline.[12] If we as a society are

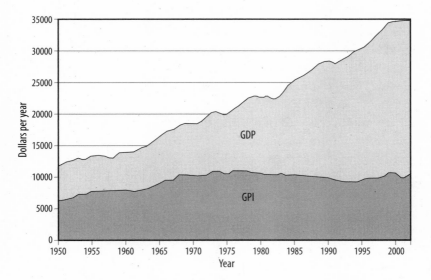

Figure 16. US Gross Domestic Product and Genuine Progress Indicators compared, 1950 to 2002. Credit: Redefining Progress

going to adjust agreeably to lower rates of energy flow — and less travel and transport — with minimal social disruption, we must begin paying more attention to the seeming intangibles of life and less to GDP and the apparent benefits of profligate energy use.

Addressing the economic, social, and political problems ensuing from the various looming peaks is no mere palliative and will require enormous collective effort. If it is to be successful, that effort must be coordinated, presumably by government, and enlist people by educating and motivating them in numbers and at a speed that has not been seen since World War II. Part of that motivation must come from a positive vision of a future worth striving toward. People will need to believe in an eventual reward for what will amount to many years of hard sacrifice. The reality is that we are approaching a time of economic contraction. Consumptive appetites that have been stoked for decades by ubiquitous advertising messages promising "more, faster, and bigger" will now have to be reined in. People will not willingly accept the new message of "less, slower, and smaller," unless they have new goals toward which to aspire. They must feel that their efforts will lead to a better world, with tangible improvements in life for themselves and their families. The massive public education campaigns that will be required must be credible, and will therefore be vastly more successful if they give people a sense of investment and involvement in formulating those goals. There is a much-abused word that describes the necessary process — *democracy.*

As another way of mitigating our paralyzing horror at seeing our society's future as one of decline in so many respects, we should ask: decline to *what?* Are we facing a complete disintegration of everything we hold dear, or merely a return to lower levels of population, complexity, and consumption? The answer, of course, is unknowable at this stage. We could indeed be at the brink of a collapse worse than any in history. Just one reference in that regard will suffice: the Millennium Ecosystem Assessment, a four-year analysis of the world's ecosystems released in 2006, in which 1,300 scientists participated, concluded that of 24 ecosystems identified as essential to human life, 15 are "being pushed beyond their sustainable limits," toward a state of collapse that may be "abrupt and potentially irre-versible."[13] The signs are not good.

Nevertheless, a decline in population, complexity, and consump-tion could, at least in theory, result in a stable society with charac-teristics that many people would find quite desirable. A reversion to the normal pattern of human existence, based on village life, ex-tended families, and local production for local consumption — especially if it were augmented by a few of the frills of the late in-dustrial period, such as global communications — could provide future generations with the kind of existence that many modern urbanites dream of wistfully.

So the overall message of this book is not necessarily one of doom — but it is one of inevitable change and the need for deliber-ate engagement with the process of change on a scale and speed be-yond anything in previous human history. Crucially: we must focus on and use the intangibles that *are not peaking* (such as ingenuity and cooperation) to address the problems arising from our overuse of substances that *are*.

Our One Great Task: The Energy Transition

As we have seen, just a few core trends have driven many others in producing the global problems we see today, and those core trends (including population growth and increasing consumption rates) themselves constellate around our ever-burgeoning use of fossil fuels. Thus, a conclusion of startling plainness presents itself: *our central survival task for the decades ahead, as individuals and as a species, must be to make a transition away from the use of fossil fuels — and to do this as peacefully, equitably, and intelligently as possible.*

At first thought, this must seem like an absurd over-simplifi-cation of the human situation. After all, the world is full of crises demanding our attention — from wars to pollution, malnutrition, land mines, human rights abuses, and soaring cancer rates. Doesn't a monomaniacal focus just on fossil fuels miss many important things?

In defense of the statement I would offer two points.

First, some problems are more critical than others. A patient may suffer simultaneously from a broken blood vessel in the brain and a broken leg. A doctor will not ignore the second problem, but since the first is immediately life-threatening, its treatment will take precedence. Globally, there are two problems whose potential consequences far outweigh all others: Climate Change and energy resource depletion. If we do nothing to dramatically curtail emissions of greenhouse gases soon, we will almost certainly set in motion the two self-reinforcing feedback loops mentioned previously — the melting of the north polar icecap, and the melting of tundra and permafrost releasing stored methane. These would lead to an averaged global warming not just of a couple of degrees, but perhaps six or more degrees over the remainder of the century. And this in turn could make much of the world uninhabitable, make agriculture impracticable in many if not most places, and result not only in the extinction of thousands or millions of other species but the deaths of hundreds of millions or billions of human beings.

If our dependence on oil, natural gas, and coal continues unabated the post-peak decline in their availability could trigger economic collapse, famine, and a general war over remaining resources. While it is certainly possible to imagine strategies to develop alternative energy sources and mandate energy conservation on a massive scale, the world is currently as reliant on hydrocarbons as it is on water, sunlight, and soil. Without oil for transportation and agriculture, without gas for heating, chemicals, and fertilizers, and without coal for power generation, the global economy would sputter to a halt. While no one envisions these fuels disappearing instantly, we can avert the worst-case scenario of global economic meltdown — with all the human tragedy that implies — only by proactively reducing our reliance on oil, gas, and coal ahead of depletion and scarcity. In other words, all that is required for the worst-case scenario to materialize is for world leaders to continue with existing policies.

These two problems are potentially lethal, first-priority ailments. If we solve them, we will then be able to devote our attention to other human dilemmas, many of which have been with us for millennia — war, disease, inequality, and so on. If we do not solve these two problems, then in a few decades our species may be in no position to make any progress whatever on other fronts; indeed, it will likely be engaged in a struggle for its very survival. We'll be literally and metaphorically burning the furniture for fuel and fighting over scraps.

My second reason for insisting that the transition from fossil fuels must take precedence over other concerns can likewise be framed in a medical metaphor: often a constellation of seemingly disparate symptoms issues from a single cause. A patient may present with symptoms of hearing loss, stomach pain, headaches, and irritability. An incompetent doctor might treat each of these symptoms separately without trying to correlate them. But if their cause is lead poisoning (which can produce all of these signs and more), then mere symptomatic treatment would be useless.

Let us unpack the metaphor. Not only are the two great crises mentioned above closely related (both Peak Oil and Climate Change issue from our dependence on fossil fuels), but, as I have already noted, many if not most of our other modern crises also constellate around fossil fuels. Even long-standing and perennial problems like economic inequality have been exacerbated by high energy-flow rates.

Pollution is no different. We humans have polluted our environments in various ways for a very long time; activities like the mining of lead and tin have produced localized devastation for centuries. However, the problem of widespread chemical pollution is a relatively new one and has grown much worse over the past decades. Many of the most dangerous pollutants happen to be fossil fuel derivatives (pesticides, plastics, and other hormone-mimicking chemicals) or by-products from the burning of coal or petroleum (nitrogen oxides and other contributors to acid rain).

War might at first seem to be a problem completely independent of our modern thirst for fossil energy sources. However, as security analyst Michael Klare has underscored in his book *Blood and Oil*,[14] many recent wars have turned on competition for control of petroleum. As oil grows scarcer in the post-peak environment, further wars and civil conflicts over the black gold are almost assured.

Moreover, the use of fossil fuels in the prosecution of war has made state-authorized mayhem far more deadly. Most modern explosives are made from fossil fuels, and even the atomic bomb — which relies on nuclear fission or fusion rather than hydrocarbons for its horrific power — depends on fossil fuels for its delivery systems.

One could go on. In summary: we have used the plentiful, cheap energy from fossil fuels, quite predictably, to expand our power over nature and one another. In doing so we have produced a laundry list of environmental and social problems. We have tried to address these one by one, but our efforts will be much more effective if directed at their common root — that is, if we end our dependence on fossil fuels.

Again, my thesis: many problems rightly deserve attention, but the problem of our dependence on fossil fuels is central to human survival, and so as long as that dependence continues to any significant extent we must make its reduction the centerpiece of all our collective efforts — whether they are efforts to feed ourselves, resolve conflicts, or maintain a functioning economy.

But this can be formulated in another, more encouraging, way. If we do focus all of our collective efforts on the central task of energy transition, we may find ourselves contributing to the solution of a wide range of problems that would be much harder to solve if we confronted each one in isolation. With a coordinated and voluntary reduction in fossil fuel consumption, we could see substantial progress in reducing many forms of environmental pollution. The decentralization of economic activity that we must pursue as transport fuels become more scarce could lead to more local jobs, more fulfilling occupations, and more robust local economies. A controlled contraction in the global oil trade could lead to a reduction of international political tensions. A planned conversion of farming to non-fossil fuel methods could mean a decline in the environmental devastation caused by agriculture and economic opportunities for millions of new farmers. Meanwhile, all of these efforts together could increase equity, community involvement, intergenerational solidarity, and the other intangible goods listed earlier.

Surely this is a future worth working toward.

The (Rude) Awakening

The subtitle of this book, "Waking Up to the Century of Declines," reflects my impression that even those of us who have been thinking about resource depletion for many years are still just beginning to awaken to its full implications. And if we are all in various stages of waking up *to* the problem, we are also waking up *from* the cultural trance of denial in which we are all embedded.[15]

This awakening is multi-dimensional. It is not just a matter of becoming intellectually and dispassionately convinced of the reality and seriousness of Climate Change, Peak Oil, or any other specific problem. Rather, it entails an emotional, cultural, and political catharsis. The biblical metaphor of scales falling from one's eyes is as apt as the pop culture meme of taking the red pill and seeing the world beyond the Matrix: in either case, waking up implies realizing that the very fabric of modern life is woven from illusion — thousands of illusions, in fact.

Holding that fabric together is one master illusion, the notion that somehow what we see around us today is *normal*. In a sense, of course, it *is* normal: the daily life experience of millions of people is normal by definition. The reality of cars, television, and fast food is calmly taken for granted; if life has been like this for decades, why shouldn't it continue, with incremental developmental changes, indefinitely? But how profoundly this "normal" life in a typical modern city differs from the lives of previous generations of humans! And the fact that it is built on the foundation of cheap fossil fuels means that future generations must and will live differently.

Again, the awakening I am describing is an ongoing visceral as well as intellectual reassessment of every facet of life — food, work, entertainment, travel, politics, economics, and more. The experience is so all-encompassing that it defies linear description. And yet we must make the attempt to describe and express it; we must turn our multi-dimensional experience into narrative, because that is how we humans process and share our experiences of the world.

The great transition of the 21st century will entail enormous adjustments on the part of every individual, family and community, and if we are to make those adjustments successfully, we will need to plan rationally. Implications and strategies will have to be explored in nearly every area of human interest — agriculture, transportation, global war and peace, public health, resource management, and on and on. Books, research studies, television documentaries, and every other imaginable form of information transferal will be required to convey needed knowledge in each of these areas. Moreover, there is the need for more than explanatory materials; we will need citizen organizations that can turn policy into action, and artists to create cultural expressions that can help fire the collective imagination. Within this whirlwind of analysis, adjustment, creativity, and transformation, perhaps there is need and space for a book that simply tries to capture the overall spirit of the time into which we are headed, that ties the multifarious upwellings of cultural change to the science of global warming and Peak Oil in some hopefully surprising and entertaining ways, and that begins to address the psychological dimension of our global transition from industrial growth to contraction and sustainability.

This book was conceived during a brief stay in a tiny village in west Cornwall in late 2006. Perhaps the bleakness of the countryside at that season is reflected in the title. However, I hope also that Cornwall's rugged beauty and its people's remaining connections with down-to-earth, pre-industrial ways of thinking and of doing things are also somehow represented, if only indirectly, in these pages.

The chapters herein are self-contained essays and while I have made every effort to put them into a helpful and logical order, readers who like to savor a book's last chapter first or to read chapters out of sequence will find that this approach works reasonably well here.

Each chapter has a story attached to it, which I will relate briefly.

"Tools with a Life of Their Own" was written in response to a penciled letter from the representative of a radical anti-technology magazine asking for an article. I wrote the requested article and sent it to the e-mail address noted in the letter. Then, when no reply was forthcoming, I sent a printout of the essay via "snail mail" to the return address on the envelope. Still no reply. To this day I do not know whether my article was rejected, whether my messages were intercepted by Federal agents, or whether the magazine's editors' ambivalence about technology rendered them unable to manage their communications responsibly. The essay was later published in the anthology *Living a Life of Value,* edited by Jason A. Merchey.[16]

"Fifty Million Farmers" is the edited text of a speech delivered in November, 2006 to the E. F. Schumacher Society (which has published the full version).[17] Over the past few months I have offered essentially the same message to the Ecological Farming Association in Asilomar, California, the National Farmers Union of Canada in Saskatoon, and the Soil Association in Cardiff, Wales. Each time I discussed the likely impacts of Peak Oil and gas for modern agriculture, and emphasized the need for dramatic, rapid reform in our global food system.

"Five Axioms of Sustainability" came from many years of frustration over the widespread, careless use of the terms *sustainable* and *sustainability*. The words would not have gained so much currency if many people were not worried that our society is in some sense *un*sustainable — i.e., that it cannot survive in its current form. Yet the terms are frequently tacked onto practices and programs (e.g., "sustainable yields" on investments) that can have no substantial impact whatever on society's ability to survive into the future. This chapter represents my effort to help refine our working definitions of these key terms. It is somewhat tougher reading than the rest of the book, and I had thought of making it an appendix; however, it is not an afterthought, but goes to the heart of every other significant discussion in the text.

Three chapters were inspired by creative works: "(*post-*)Hydrocarbon Aesthetics" came from a visit to an Arts and Crafts museum exhibit; "Parrots and Peoples" followed my viewing of the documentary film *The Wild Parrots of Telegraph Hill;* and "Population, Resources, and Human Idealism" was my response to the Broadway musical, *Urinetown*. In each case, the result was not a review in the usual sense, but rather an exploration of ideas relating to the theme of this book.

"The Psychology of Peak Oil and Climate Change" arose from scores of conversations with people about their experience of the awakening process. Clearly, humanity is addicted to fossil fuels, and this essay offers some suggestions on what sorts of group therapy might help us kick the habit.

I was inspired to write "Bridging Peak Oil and Climate Change Activism" after participating in two days of meetings in San Francisco in the fall of 2006, in which prominent Climate Change and Peak Oil activists attempted to form common strategies. It was my impression that the discussants often did not understand one another well, hence my effort to sort out the issues and point toward potential paths for better communication and coordination of efforts.

"Boomers' Last Chance?" is both a personal *mea culpa* and a plea to the other members of my demographic cohort. We may belong to the peak generation, in that we will have consumed something like half the world's nonrenewable resources during our lifetime. We have enjoyed an unprecedented party, but the privilege of having a place at this greatest banquet in history implies an enormous responsibility to future generations.

"A Letter From the Future," originally published in 2000, is of the genre of the classic novel *Looking Backward: 2000–1887* by Edward Bellamy, which imagined, from that writer's perspective in the late 19th century, life in our time. Bellamy's vision inevitably proved myopic: while *Looking Backward* was popular and influential (it sold over a million copies and inspired many Progressive reforms throughout the next two decades), it did not successfully anticipate the world of the early 21st century. Bellamy saw our era as one in which government would control the means of production and divide wealth equally between all people and in which all citizens would receive a college education and be given freedom in choosing a career, from which they would retire at age 45. In short, Bellamy foresaw a socialist utopia and entirely missed the realities of globalization, sweat shops, and environmental devastation. My own effort is likely to be just as inaccurate — though while Bellamy's failed by being too sanguine, I hope mine proves too dire.

"Talking Ourselves to Extinction" is a meditation on the power of language — a tool whose development and use has shaped us as a species. Cultural evolution occurred primarily because language enabled us to coordinate our efforts to respond quickly to environmental challenges and opportunities. Words have given us power over nature, and have given some human groups power over others. Today, if we are to survive, we must change our collective behavior radically and swiftly; only our species' unique linguistic talent is capable of orchestrating such an evolutionary shift. This book is a testament of hope that words can help us recognize the limits of nature, and the limits of power itself, before it is too late.

On Technology, Agriculture, and the Arts

1

Tools with a Life of Their Own

NEARLY EVERYONE complains from time to time that our tools have become Sorcerer's Apprentices; that we have come to serve our machines instead of the other way around; and that, increasingly, our lives are regimented as if we ourselves were mere cogs in a vast mechanism utterly beyond our control.

We are not the first people to feel this way: criticism of technology has a history. The Luddites of early 19th-century England were among the first to raise their voices — and hammers! — against the dehumanizing side effects of mechanization. As industrialization proceeded decade-by-decade — from powered looms to steam shovels, jet planes, and electric toothbrushes — objections to the accelerating, mindless adoption of new technologies waxed erudite. During the past century, books by Lewis Mumford, Jacques Ellul, Ivan Illich, Kirkpatrick Sale, Stephanie Mills, Chellis Glendinning, Jerry Mander, John Zerzan, and Derrick Jensen, among others, have helped generations of readers understand how and why our tools have come to enslave us, colonizing our minds as well as our daily routines.

These authors reminded us that tools, far from being morally neutral, are amplifiers of human purposes; therefore each tool carries its inventor's original intent inherent within it. We can use a revolver to hammer nails, but it works better as a machine for the swift commission of mayhem; and the more handguns we have around, the more likely it is for inevitable, daily personal conflicts to go ballistic. Thus, as clashes over human purposes form the core of ethical and political disputes, technology itself, as it proliferates, must inevitably become the subject of an increasing array of social controversies. Battles over technology concern nothing less than the shape and future of society.

In principle, those battles, if not the scholarly discussions about them, reach all the way back to the Neolithic era, and perhaps to our harnessing of fire tens of thousands of years ago. Lewis Mumford drew a through-line emphasizing how modern megatechnologies are externalizations of a social machine that originated in the pristine states of the Bronze Age:

> The inventors of nuclear bombs, space rockets, and computers are the pyramid builders of our own age: psychologically inflated by a similar myth of unqualified power, boasting through their science of their increasing omnipotence, if not omniscience, moved by obsessions and compulsions no less irrational than those of earlier absolute systems: particularly the notion that the system itself must be expanded, at whatever the eventual cost.[1]

John Zerzan goes further, asserting that it is the human tendencies to abstract and manipulate, which are at the heart of our tool-making ability, that cut us off from our innate connections with the natural world, and therefore obscure our own inherent nature.[2]

This effort to show how our current technological crisis is rooted in ancient patterns is certainly helpful. But it is important also to keep in mind the fact that the discussion about mechanization's nasty side effects has intensified relatively recently, due to the *scale* of technology's intrusion into our lives and its toll upon the environment having grown enormously in just the past two centuries.

Some techno-critics have sought to explain this recent explosion in the power and variety of our tools by tying it to developments in philosophy (Cartesian dualism) or economics (capitalism). Strangely, few of the critics have discussed at any length the role of fossil

fuels in the industrial revolution. That is, they have consistently focused their attention on tools' impacts on society and nature, and
on the political conditions and ideologies that enabled their adoption, rather than on the fact that most of the new tools that have appeared during the past two centuries are of a kind previously rare,
deriving the energy for their operation not from muscle power, but
from the burning of fuels.

Mumford, one of my favorite authors, devoted only one comment on one page of his 700-page, two-volume masterpiece *The
Myth of the Machine,* to coal, and neither "petroleum" nor "oil" appears in the index of either volume.[3] My own 1996 book, *A New
Covenant with Nature,* which was largely devoted to a critique of
industrialism, does no better: "coal," "oil," and "energy" are absent
from its index.[4]

And yet it appears to me now that, in assessing and understanding technology and its effects on people and nature, it is at least as
important to pay attention to the energy that drives our tools as to
the tools themselves and the surrounding political-ideological matrix. In short, we who have been criticizing the technological society, using the tools of historical analysis, have missed at least half the
story we are attempting to weave when we fail to notice the energetic evolution of tools.

This chapter is a brief attempt to make up for these oversights. It
will also discuss why the impending peak in global oil production
will pull the plug on the kind of "progress" we have come to expect,
providing an historic opportunity to reshape humanity's relations
with technology and with nature.

Classy Tools

It is helpful for our purposes here to classify tools according to their
energy inputs. The following four categories, outlined in my book
The Party's Over,[5] correspond very roughly to four major water-
sheds in social evolution:

   A. Tools that require only human energy for their manufacture and use. Examples: stone spearheads and arrowheads,

grinding tools, baskets, and animal-skin clothing. These sorts of tools are found in all hunter-gatherer societies.

B. Tools that require an external power source for their manufacture, but human power for their use. Examples: all basic metal tools, such as knives, metal armor, and coins. These tools were the basis of the early agricultural civilizations centered in Mesopotamia, China, Egypt, and Rome.

C. Tools that require only human energy for their manufacture, but harness an external energy source in their use. Examples: the wooden plow drawn by draft animals, the sailboat, the fire drill, the windmill, the water mill. The fire drill was used by hunter-gatherers, and the wooden plow and sailboat were developed in early agricultural societies; the windmill and water mill appeared at later stages of social evolution.

D. Tools that require an external energy source for their manufacture and also harness or use an external energy source. Examples: the steel plow, the gun, the steam engine, the internal combustion engine, the jet engine, the nuclear reactor, the hydroelectric turbine, the photovoltaic panel, the wind turbine, and all electrical devices. These tools and tool systems are the foundation of modern industrial societies — in fact, they define them.

For thousands of years, human beings have engaged in a constant struggle to harness extrasomatic energy (that is, energy from sources other than the food they eat). Until recently, such energy came mostly from the capture of work performed by animal muscles. In the US, as recently as 1850, domesticated animals — horses, oxen, and mules — were responsible for over two thirds of the physical work supporting the economy. Today the percentage is negligible: virtually all work is done by fuel-fed machines. Slavery was a strategy for capturing human muscle power, and the end of most formal slavery during the 19th century was more or less inevitable when Class D tools became cheaper to own and keep than human slaves — or domesticated animals, for that matter.

In early civilizations, agricultural workers sought to capture a surplus of solar energy on a yearly basis by plowing and reaping, and between 70 and 90 percent of the population had to work at farming in order to provide enough of a surplus to support the rest of the social edifice, including the warrior, priestly, and administrative classes. The extraction of coal, and especially of oil and natural gas — substances representing millions of years of accumulation of past biotic energy — has often provided a spectacular net-energy profit. With fossil fuels and modern machinery, only two percent of the population now needs to farm in order to support the rest of society, enabling the flourishing of a growing middle class composed of a dizzying array of specialists.

Increasing specialization was also enabled by a flourishing of differing types of machines, and over the past few decades that differentiation was itself in turn fueled (quite literally) by the availability of cheap energy to make the machines go. Labor productivity increased relentlessly, not because people worked longer or harder, but because they had access to an increasing array of powerful extrasomatically powered tools.

The availability of Class D tools produced excitement and wonder — initially among the few people wealthy enough to own them, and also among the crafty

Lewis Hines's classic 1920 photo of a power-house mechanic was likely an inspiration for Charlie Chaplin's set designs for "Modern Times." The image and the film portray humans in industrial settings as slaves to their machines. Credit: Lewis Hines

and highly motivated inventors available for hire. These tools were, in a sense, alive: they consumed a kind of food, in the form of coal or oil, and had their own internal metabolism. Gradually, as mechanized production showed itself capable of producing more gadgets than could possibly be soaked up by the wealthy elites, the latter devised the strategy of creating a consumer society in which anyone could own labor-saving machinery. The rank and file were soon persuaded of the dream of eliminating drudgery. And, due to the scale of the energies being unleashed, the fulfillment of that dream seemed well within reach.

That scale is difficult to comprehend without using familiar examples. Think for a moment of the effort required to push, for only a few feet, an automobile that has run out of gas. Now imagine pushing it 20 miles. This is, of course, the service provided by a single gallon of gasoline, which contains the energy equivalent to at least six weeks of human labor (much more than this by some accounts). The amount of gasoline, diesel, and kerosene fuels used in the US in one day has the energy equivalence of roughly 20,000,000 person/years of work. If the building of the Great Pyramid required 10,000 people working for 20 years, then the petroleum-based energy used in the US on an average day could — in principle, given the necessary stone and machinery — build 100 Great Pyramids. Of course, we don't use our oil for this purpose: instead we use it mostly to push millions of metal cars along roadways so that we can get to and from jobs, malls, restaurants, and video rental stores.

With computers and cybernetics, we managed to create tools with not just a life, but a *mind* of their own. Now our tools not only "breathe," "eat," and do physical work; they also "think." Increasingly we find ourselves in synthetic, self-regulating (if not yet self-replicating) environments — shopping malls, airports, office buildings — in which non-human multicelled biota are present only as ornaments or pests; in which human work consists only of the few tasks for which we have not yet invented profitable automatic surrogates. The wonder of seeing drudgery eliminated is accompanied by the nuisance of being managed and bossed about by machines, and of being rendered helpless by mechanical failures or — horror of horrors — power outages.

It's the Energy, Silly

What does it take to enable these techno-miracles? It takes 85 million barrels of oil per day globally, as well as millions of tons of coal and billions of cubic feet of natural gas. The supply network for these fuels is globe-spanning and awesome. Yet, from the standpoint of the end user, this network is practically invisible and easily taken for granted. We flip the switch, pump the gas, or turn up the thermostat with hardly a thought to the processes of extraction we draw upon, or the environmental horrors they entail.

The machines themselves have become so sophisticated, their services so seductive, that they are equivalent to magic. Few people fully understand the inner workings of any given tool, and different tools require their own unique teams of specialists for their design and repair. But what is more important, in the process of becoming dependent upon them, we have become almost a different species as compared to our recent ancestors.

Eniac (short for Electronic Numerical Integrator and Computer), unveiled in 1946, was the first large-scale, electronic, digital computer able to be reprogrammed to solve a range of computing problems. Credit: US Army

Infrastructure Matters

To understand *how* we have become so different, how different we have become, and also how the end of cheap extrasomatic energy is likely to impact us and the society in which we are embedded, it is helpful to draw another lesson from cultural anthropology.

Comparative studies have consistently shown that human societies are best classified on the basis of their members' means of obtaining food. Thus we commonly speak of hunting-and-gathering societies, horticultural societies, agricultural societies, fishing societies, herding societies, and industrial societies. The point is, if you know how people get their food, you will reliably be able to predict most of the rest of their social forms — their decision-making and child-rearing customs, spiritual practices, and so on.

Of course, from a biological point of view, food is energy. And so what we are saying (once again, but in a slightly different way) is that understanding energy sources is essential to understanding human societies.

Anthropologist Marvin Harris identified three basic elements that are present in every human society:

- *infrastructure,* which consists of the means of obtaining and processing necessary energy and materials from nature—i.e., the means of production;
- *structure,* which consists of human-to-human decision-making and resource-allocating activities; and
- *superstructure,* consisting of the ideas, rituals, ethics, and myths that serve to explain the universe and coordinate human behavior.[6]

Change at any of these levels can affect the others: the emergence of a new religion or a political revolution, for example, can change people's lives in real, significant ways. However, the fact that so many cultural forms seem consistently to cluster around ways of obtaining food suggests that *fundamental* cultural change occurs at the infrastructural level: if people switch, for example, from hunting to planting, or from planting to herding, their politics and spirituality are bound to shift as well, and probably in profound ways.

The industrial revolution represented one of history's pivotal infrastructural shifts; everything about human society changed as a result. This revolution did *not* come about primarily because of religious or political developments, but because a few prior inventions (steel, gears, and a primitive steam engine — i.e., Class B and C and simple Class D tools) came together in the presence of an abundant new energy source: fossil fuels — first coal, then oil and natural gas. Ideas (such as Cartesian dualism, capitalism, Calvinism, and Marxism), rather than driving the transformation, achieved prominence because they served useful functions within a flow of events emanating from infrastructural necessity.

What Hath Hydrocarbon Wrought?
What have been the structural and superstructural impacts of industrialism?

Because only a reduced portion of the population is required to work the land in order to produce food-energy (now with tractors and harvesters rather than oxen), a large majority of the populace has lost direct connection with the land and with the cycles of nature. If hunters get their food-energy from hunting, we get ours from shopping at the supermarket.

The ensuing proliferation, first of factory work and later of specialized occupations, has led to the development of universal compulsory public education and the idea of the "job" — a notion that most people today take for granted, but that seems strange, demeaning, and confining to people in non-industrial cultures.

With the expansion of the educated middle class, simple monarchical forms of government soon ceased to be defensible. By the latter part of the 18th century, a trend was well established, within incipient industrial nations, of revolution and the widespread and growing expectation of democratic participation in governance — though of course that expectation was quickly hijacked by the *nouveau* mercantile elites. Somewhat later, the economic exploitation of labor that typified both previous agricultural civilizations and the new industrial states also became the target of revolution; once again, the primary effect of revolution was primarily merely to rearrange the deck chairs: people's actual daily work and psychic life were still being shaped by machines, and, at a deeper level, the energy sources that propelled them.

We must remember that industrialism followed on the heels of the European takeover of the resources and labor of most of the rest of the world during centuries of conquest and colonialism. Thus the experience and expectation of economic growth had already insinuated itself into the minds of members of the European merchant class before industrialism took hold. Once the fuel revolution began, with vastly more energy available per capita, economic activity achieved seemingly perpetual exponential growth, and economic theories emerged not only to explain this growth in terms of "markets," but to affirm that now, because of markets, growth was necessary, inevitable, and unending. World without end, amen. Fractional-reserve banking, based on the wonder of compound interest, served as the fiscal embodiment of these new expectations. In effect, within the minds of society's managers and policy makers, faith in technology and markets supplanted previous religious faith in the hallucinatory agricultural and herding deities that had presided over Western civilization for the previous couple of millennia.

In the early 20th century, as mechanized production mushroomed to swamp existing demand for manufactured products (among people who mostly still lived rurally and fairly self-sufficiently), elites began experimenting with mass propaganda in the form of advertising and public relations. Later, television would dramatically increase the effectiveness of these efforts, which amounted to nothing less than the regimentation of the human imagination according to the demands of the industrial system.

George Stephenson's "Rocket," built in 1829, was the world's first steam locomotive, which opened the way to fossil-fueled travel and transport. Credit: Public Domain

Since women were now needed both as consumers and workers in order to continue the perpetual expansion of that system, feminism (via the destruction of old domestic roles and the promotion of new ambitions and consumer tastes) became an inevitable byproduct.

In short, just as we would predict on the basis of the theory of infrastructural determinism, when fossil fuels deeply altered humanity's means of obtaining sustenance from the Earth, everything about human society changed — from child rearing to politics; from cultural myths to personal dreams.

Of course, many of these changes were destructive both of people and nature. And so, while many of the political struggles of the 20th century centered on questions of the distribution of power and wealth (as had been the case since the first agricultural surpluses were laid aside over 7,000 years ago), many of those struggles also

CAN SCIENCE MAKE US LIVE FOREVER?

This cover of *Modern Mechanix and Inventions* from June, 1936, typifies the techno-optimism of the mid-20th century. Credit: Public Domain.

grew from efforts to control technology's caustic impacts, which were linked by social critics both to tools themselves and to people's attitudes toward them.

Technological politics focused on a range of issues: nuclear weapons and nuclear power, polluting chemicals, ozone-destroying chlorofluorocarbons, greenhouse gases, and the genetic engineering of food, to name only a few familiar examples. The most radical of the techno-critics were inspired by the writings of anthropologists such as Stanley Diamond, who evinced profound admiration for the world's remaining hunter-gatherers. For the anarcho-primitivist philosopher John Zerzan, *all* technology is damaging, debauched, destructive, and demeaning, and only a return to our primordial, pre-linguistic, pre-technic condition will enable us to recover fully our innate freedom and spontaneity.[7]

On the other hand, techno-optimists proclaimed that humanity was in the process of overthrowing age-old limits of every kind — to population growth, levels of consumption, ease of movement, quickness of communication, access to information, and so on.

But the techno-critics and the techno-boosters, from the mildest to the most extreme, have all tended to assume that, for decades hence, barring intervention, humanity will pursue a continued trajectory of technological change: the only thing that could thwart this ongoing "progress" would be the awakening of a new moral sensibility (misplaced, in the view of the techno-boosters) leading humans to reject technology, entirely or in part.

Peak Oil and the Limits of Technology

With the discourse on Peak Oil that has commenced since the beginning of the new millennium has come a focus on energy as the determining factor in social evolution — rather than technology *per se,* or ideas, or political struggles. And with that shift has also come the sense that resource limits will eventually drive basic cultural change — rather than moral persuasion, mass enlightenment, or some new invention.

As oil and gas prices rise, signaling the start of the peaking period, we continue to see the rollout of new inventions in the form of the latest iPhone, the next generation of nuclear bombs, improved surveillance tools, and so on. However, there is also evidence that the stream of new inventions, like the global stream of oil, is starting to dry up.

Physicist Jonathan Huebner of the Pentagon's Naval Air Warfare Center in China Lake, California, has for several years been studying the pace of technological change and invention, using innovations catalogued in *The History of Science and Technology.* After applying some elaborate mathematics, he has concluded that the rate of invention of significantly new and different tools peaked in 1873 and has been dwindling gradually since then. Huebner

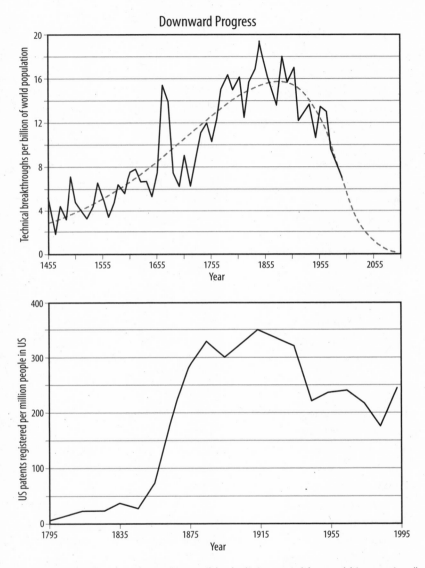

Figure 18. Credit: J. Huebner, "A possible declining trend for world innovation," *Technological Forecasting and Social Change,* Vol. 72, Issue 8, October 1, 2005

calculates our current rate of innovation at seven important technological developments per billion people per year — about the same rate as prevailed in Europe in 1600. If the trend continues, by 2024 the innovation rate will have declined to that of the Dark Ages.[8]

Assuming Huebner is right, it would seem that the 19th-century adoption of fossil fuels led to an early-peaking wave of invention, and we are living on its trailing edge. As fossil fuels peak and decline, we are unlikely to see another such burst of similar kinds or degrees of innovation; instead, we will see *adaptation* to a lower-energy cultural environment. And that adaptation may occur by way of versions of older cultural patterns that resulted from previous generations' responses to similar levels of available energy.

Peak Oil will be a fundamental cultural watershed, at least as important as the industrial revolution or the development of agriculture. Yet few mainstream commentators see it that way. They discuss the likelihood of energy price spikes and try to calculate how much economic havoc will result from them. Always the solution is technology: solar or wind and maybe a bit of hydrogen for green-tinged idealists; nuclear, tar sands, methane hydrates, and coal-to-liquids for hard-headed, pro-growth economists and engineers; Tesla's free-energy magnetic generators for the gullible fringe dwellers.

But technology cannot solve the underlying dilemma we face as a result of our application of fossil fuels to every human problem or desire. We are growing our population, destroying habitat, undermining global climatic stability, and depleting resources in ways and at rates that cannot be mitigated by *any* new tool or energy source. The only way forward that does not end with the extinction of humanity and thousands or millions of other species is a scaling back of the entire human project — in terms both of human numbers and per-capita rates of consumption.

How dramatic a pullback are we talking about? No one knows. It depends to a large degree on how we manage the inevitable collapse in financial and governance systems, and whether the nations of the world can be persuaded to adopt a global Oil Depletion Protocol; or whether instead they fight mercilessly over the last petroleum reserves until even the "winners" are utterly spent and the resources in dispute have been used up or destroyed in the conflict itself.

In the worst case, Zerzan's ideal of a return to hunting and gathering may be realized — though not by moral choice, but by cruel fate.

If Class D tools fueled by cheap oil eliminated drudgery, life without abundant extrasomatic energy will imply more labor — certainly for food production. The return of slavery is a frighteningly real possibility. Such nightmare scenarios can only be averted by careful, hard, cooperative work.

Staring at Techno-Collapse

In the meantime, what should we expect and what should we do?

Realistically, I think we can expect to see some of the worst excesses of human history, but perhaps only briefly and in certain places. Within a few decades the governmental and corporate structures capable of perpetrating such outrages will have crumbled for lack of fuel. We can also anticipate — and participate in — localized cooperative attempts to reorganize society at a smaller scale.

Under the circumstances, efforts to *try* to bring industrialism to ruin prematurely seem to be pointless and wrongheaded: ruin will come soon enough on its own. Better to invest time and effort in personal and community preparedness. Enhance your survival prospects. Learn practical skills, including the manufacture and use of Paleolithic tools. Learn to understand and repair (as much as possible) existing tools — including water pumps, farm implements, and woodworking tools — that are likely still to be useful when there is no gasoline or electricity.

Preserve whatever is beautiful, sane, and intelligent. That includes scientific and cultural knowledge, and examples of human achievement in the arts. Nobody can preserve it all, or even a substantial portion; choose what appeals to you. A great deal of it is currently captured on media with dubious survival prospects — magnetic disc or tape, compact laser disc, or acid-soaked paper. If someone doesn't make the effort, the best of what we have achieved over the past centuries and decades will be gone along with the worst.

In the best instance, the next generations will find themselves in a low-energy regime in which moral lessons from the fossil-fuel era and its demise have been seared into cultural memory. Like the Native Americans, who learned from the Pleistocene extinctions that over-hunting results in famine, they will have discovered that growth is not always good, that modest material goals are usually better for everyone in the long run than extravagant ones, and that every technology has a hidden cost. There is no free lunch. One hopes that, like the Iroquois, who long ago concluded that fighting over scarce land and resources only means the endless perpetuation of violence, they will also have learned the methods and culture of peacemaking.

We humans tend to learn really tough lessons only by bitter experience. These are tough lessons indeed. If we learn them, perhaps the bitter experience of addicting ourselves to fossil fuels and then having to go cold turkey will not have been entirely pointless.

2

Fifty Million Farmers

THERE WAS A TIME not so long ago when famine was an expected, if not accepted, part of life. Until the 19th century — whether in China, France, India, or Britain — food came almost entirely from local sources and harvests were variable. In good years, there was plenty — enough for seasonal feasts and for storage in anticipation of winter and hard times to come. In bad years, starvation cut down the poorest and the weakest — the very young, the old, and the sickly. Sometimes bad years followed one upon another, reducing the size of the population by several percent. This was the *normal* condition of life in pre-industrial societies, and it persisted for thousands of years.[1]

Today in America, such a state of affairs is hard to imagine. Food is so cheap and plentiful that obesity is a far more widespread concern than hunger. The average mega-supermarket stocks an impressive array of exotic foods from across the globe, and even staples are typically trucked from hundreds of miles away. Many people in America did go hungry during the Great Depression, but those were times that only the elderly can recall. In the current regime, the desperately poor may experience chronic malnutrition and may miss meals, but for most the dilemma is finding time in the day's hectic schedule to go to the grocery store or to cook. As a result, fast-food restaurants proliferate: the fare may not be particularly nutritious, but even an hour's earnings at minimum wage will buy a meal or two. The average American family spent 20 percent of its income on food in 1950; today the figure is 10 percent.[2]

While this is an extraordinary situation, it is the only one that most Americans alive today have ever experienced, and so we tend to assume that it will continue indefinitely. However, there are reasons to think that our current anomalous abundance of inexpensive food may be only temporary; if so, present and future generations may become acquainted with that old, formerly familiar but unwelcome houseguest — famine.

The following are the four principal bases (there are others) for this gloomy forecast.

The first factor has to with *looming fuel shortages*. This is a subject I have written about extensively elsewhere, so I shall not repeat myself in any detail. Suffice it to say that the era of cheap oil and natural gas is coming to a crashing end, with global oil production projected to peak around the year 2010 and North American natural gas extraction rates already in decline. These events will have enormous implications for America's petroleum-dependent food system.

Modern industrial agriculture has been described as a method of using soil to turn petroleum and gas into food. We use natural gas to make fertilizer. We use oil to fuel farm machinery and power irrigation pumps, as a feedstock for pesticides and herbicides, in the maintenance of animal operations, in crop storage and drying, and for transportation of farm inputs and outputs. Agriculture accounts for about 17 percent of the US annual energy budget; it is the single largest consumer of petroleum products as compared to other industries. By comparison, the US military, in all of its operations, uses less than half that amount. About 350 gallons (1,500 liters) of oil equivalents are required to feed each American each year, and every calorie of food produced requires, on average, ten calories of fossil-fuel inputs. This is a food system profoundly vulnerable, at every level, to fuel shortages and skyrocketing prices. And both are inevitable.

An attempt to make up for fuel shortfalls by producing more biofuels — ethanol, butanol, and biodiesel — will put even more pressure on the food system, and will likely result in a competition between food and fuel uses of land and the other resources needed for agricultural production. Already 14 percent of the US corn crop is devoted to making ethanol, and that proportion is expected to rise to one quarter, based solely on existing projects-in-development and government mandates.[3]

The second factor potentially leading to famine is *a shortage of farmers*. Much of the success of industrial agriculture lies in its labor efficiency: far less human work is required to produce a given amount of food today than was the case decades ago (the actual fraction, comparing the year 2000 with 1900, is about one seventh). But that very success implies a growing vulnerability. We don't need as many farmers, as a percentage of the population, as we used to; so, throughout the past century, most farming families — including hundreds of thousands and perhaps millions that would have preferred to maintain their rural, self-sufficient way of life — were forced to move to cities and find jobs. Today so few people farm that vital knowledge of *how* to farm is disappearing. The average age of American farmers is over 55 and approaching 60. The proportion of principal farm operators younger than 35 has dropped from 15.9 percent in 1982 to 5.8 percent in 2002. Of all the dismal statistics I know, these are surely among the most frightening. Who will be growing our food 20 years from now? With less oil and gas available, we will need far *more* knowledge and muscle power devoted to food production, and thus far more people on the farm, than we have currently.

The third worrisome trend is *an increasing scarcity of fresh water*. Over 80 percent of fresh water consumed nationally goes toward agriculture. California's Central Valley, which produces the substantial bulk of the nation's fruits, nuts, and vegetables, receives virtually no rainfall during summer months and relies overwhelmingly on irrigation. But the snowpack on the Sierras, which provides much of that irrigation water, is declining, and the aquifer that supplies much of the rest is being drawn down at many times its recharge rate. If these trends continue, the Central Valley may be incapable of producing food in any substantial quantities within two or three decades. Other parts of the country are similarly overspending their water budgets, and very little is being done to deal with this looming catastrophe.

Fourth and finally, there is the problem of *global Climate Change*. Often the phrase used for this is "global warming," which implies only that the world's average temperature will be increasing by a couple of degrees or more over the next few decades. The much greater problem for farmers is destabilization of weather patterns. We face not just a warmer climate, but *climate chaos:* droughts, floods, and stronger storms in general (hurricanes, cyclones, tornadoes, hail storms) — unpredictable weather of all kinds. Farmers depend on relatively consistent seasonal patterns of rain and sun, cold and heat; a climate shift can spell the end of farmers' ability to grow a crop in a given region, and even a single freak storm can destroy an entire year's production. Given the fact that modern American agriculture has become highly centralized due to cheap transport and economies of scale (almost the entire national spinach crop, for example, comes from a single valley in California), the damage from that freak storm is today potentially continental or even global in scope. We have embarked on a century in which, increasingly, freakish weather is normal.

I am not pointing out these problems, and their likely consequences, in order to cause panic. As I propose below, there is a solution to at least two of these dilemmas, one that may also help us address the remaining two. It is not a simple or easy strategy and it will require a coordinated and sustained national effort. But in addition to averting famine, this strategy may permit us to solve a host of other, seemingly unrelated social and environmental problems.

Intensifying Food Production

In order to get a better grasp of the problems and the solution being proposed, it is essential that we understand how our present exceptional situation of cheap abundance came about. In order to do that, we must go back not just a few decades, but at least ten thousand years.

The origins of agriculture are shrouded in mystery, though

archaeologists have been whittling away at that mystery for decades. We know that horticulture (gardening) began independently at somewhat different periods, in at least three regions — the Middle East, Southeast Asia, and Central America. Following the end of the last Ice Age, roughly 12,000 years ago, much of humanity experienced a centuries-long food crisis brought on by overhunting the megafauna that had been at the center of the human diet. The subsequent domestication of plants and animals brought relative food security, as well as the ability to support larger and more sedentary populations.

Compared to hunting and gathering, horticulture intensified the process of obtaining food — that is, it produced more food per unit of land, using more labor. Intensification (because it led to increased population density — i.e., more mouths to feed), then led to the need for even more intensification: thus horticulture (gardening) eventually led to agriculture (field cropping). The latter produced still more food per unit of land, which enabled more population growth, which meant still more demand for food. We are describing a classic self-reinforcing feedback loop.

As a social regime, horticulture did not represent a decisive break with hunting and gathering. Just as women had previously participated in essential productive activities by foraging for plants and hunting small animals, they now played a prominent role in planting, tending, and harvesting the garden — activities that were all compatible with caring for infants and small children. Thus women's status remained relatively high in most horticultural societies. Seasonal surpluses were relatively small and there was no full-time division of labor.

But as agriculture developed — with field crops, plows, and draft animals — societies inevitably mutated in response. Plowing fields was men's work; women were forced to stay at home and lost social power. Larger seasonal surpluses required management as well as protection from raiders; full-time managers and specialists in violence proliferated as a result. Societies became multi-layered: wealthy ruling classes (which had never existed among hunter-gatherers, and were rare among gardeners) sat atop an economic pyramid that came to include scribes, soldiers, and religious functionaries, and that was supported at its base by the vastly more numerous peasants — who produced all the food, for themselves and everyone else as well. Writing, mathematics, metallurgy, and, ultimately, the trappings of modern life as we know it thus followed not so much from planting in general, as from agriculture in particular.

As important an instance of intensification as agriculture was, in many respects it pales in comparison with what has occurred within the past century or so, with the application of fossil fuels to farming. Petroleum-fed tractors replaced horses and oxen, freeing up more land to grow food for far more people. The Haber-Bosch process for synthesizing ammonia from fossil fuels, invented just prior to World War I, has doubled the amount of nitrogen available to green plants — with nearly all of that increase going directly to food crops. New hybrid plant varieties also led to higher yields. Technologies for food storage improved radically. And fuel-fed transport systems enabled local surpluses to be sold not just regionally, but nationally and even globally. Through all of these strategies, we have developed the wherewithal to feed seven times the population that existed at the beginning of the Industrial Revolution. And, in the process, we have made farming uneconomical and unattractive to all but a few.

That's the broad, global overview. In America, whose history as an independent nation begins at the dawn of the industrial era, the story of agriculture comprises three distinct periods:

The Expansion Period (1600 to 1920): Increases in food production during these three centuries came simply from putting more land into production; technological change played only a minor role.

The Mechanization Period (1920 to 1970): In this half-century, technological advances issuing from cheap, abundant fossil-fuel energy resulted in a dramatic increase in productivity as measured by output per worker hour. Meanwhile, farm machinery, pesticides, herbicides, irrigation, new hybrid crops, and synthetic fertilizers allowed for the doubling and tripling of crop production per acre. Also during this time, US Department of Agriculture policy began favoring larger farms (the average US farm size grew from 100 acres in 1930 to almost 500 acres by 1990), and production for export.

The Saturation Period (1970-present): In recent decades, the application of still greater amounts of energy has produced smaller relative increases in crop yields; meanwhile, an ever-growing amount of energy is being expended just to maintain the functioning of the overall system. For example, about ten percent of the energy in agriculture is used to offset the negative effects of soil erosion, while increasing amounts of pesticides must be sprayed each year as pests develop resistances. In short, strategies that had recently produced dramatic increases in productivity became subject to the law of diminishing returns.

While we were achieving miracles of productivity, agriculture's impact on the natural world was also growing; indeed it is now the single greatest source of human damage to the global environment. That damage takes a number of forms: erosion and salinization of soils; deforestation (a strategy for bringing more land into cultivation); fertilizer runoff (which ultimately creates enormous "dead zones" around the mouths of many rivers); other agrochemical pollution of water and soil; loss of biodiversity; and fresh water scarcity.

In short, we created unprecedented abundance while ignoring the long-term consequences of our actions. This is more than a little reminiscent of how some previous agricultural societies — the Greeks, Babylonians, and Romans — destroyed soil and habitat in their mania to feed growing urban populations, and collapsed as a result.

Fortunately, during the past century or two we have also developed the disciplines of archaeology and ecology, which teach us how and why those ancient societies failed, and how the diversity of the web of life sustains us. In principle, if we avail ourselves of this knowledge, we need not mindlessly repeat yet again the time-worn tale of catastrophic civilizational collapse.

The 21st Century: De-Industrialization

How might we avoid such a fate?

Surely the dilemmas we have outlined above are understood by the managers of the current industrial food system. They must have some solutions in mind.

Indeed they do, and, perhaps predictably, those solutions involve a further intensification of the food production process. Since we cannot achieve much by applying more energy directly to that process, the most promising strategy on the horizon seems to be the genetic engineering of new crop varieties. If, for example, we could design crops to grow with less water, or in unfavorable climate and soil conditions, we could perhaps find our way out of the current mess.

Unfortunately, there are some flaws with this plan. Our collective experience with genetically modifying crops so far shows that glowing promises of higher yields, or of the reduced need for herbicides, have seldom been fulfilled. At the same time, new genetic technologies carry with them the potential for horrific unintended consequences in the forms of negative impacts on human health and the integrity of ecosystems. We have been gradually modifying plants and animals through selective breeding for millennia, but new gene-splicing techniques enable the re-mixing of genomes in ways and to degrees impossible heretofore. One serious error could result in biological tragedy on an unprecedented scale.

In France, the *potager,* or kitchen garden, has a long tradition and is still extremely popular. Credit: Jean-Noël Lafargue

Yet even if future genetically modified commercial crops prove to be much more successful than past ones, and even if we manage to avert a genetic apocalypse, the means of producing and distributing genetically engineered seeds is itself reliant on the very fuel-fed industrial system that is in question.

Is it possible, then, that a solution lies in another direction altogether — perhaps in deliberately de-industrializing production, but doing so intelligently, using information we have gained from the science of ecology, as well as from traditional and indigenous farming methods, in order to reduce environmental impacts while maintaining total yields at a level high enough to avert widespread famine?

This is not an entirely new idea (the organic and ecological farming movements have been around for decades), but up to this point the managers of the current system have resisted it. This is no doubt largely because those managers are heavily influenced by giant corporations that profit from centralized industrial production for distant markets. Nevertheless, the fact that we have reached the end of the era of cheap oil and gas demands that we re-examine the potential costs and benefits of our current trajectory and its alternatives.

I believe we must and can de-industrialize agriculture. The general outline of what I mean by de-industrialization is simple enough: a radical reduction of fossil fuel inputs to agriculture, accompanied by an increase in labor inputs and a reduction of transport, with production being devoted primarily to local consumption.

Once again, fossil fuel depletion almost ensures that this *will* happen. But at the same time, it is fairly obvious that if we don't *plan* for de-industrialization, the result could be catastrophic. It's worth taking a moment to think about how events might unfold if the process occurs without intelligent management, driven simply by oil and gas depletion.

Facing high fuel prices, family farms would declare bankruptcy in record numbers. Older farmers (the majority, in other words) would probably choose simply to retire, whether they could afford to or not. However, giant corporate farms would also confront rising costs — which they would pass along to consumers by way of dramatically higher food prices.

Yields would begin to decline — in fits and starts — as weather anomalies and water shortages affected one crop after another.

Meanwhile, people in the cities would also feel the effects of skyrocketing energy prices. Entire industries would falter, precipitating a general economic collapse. Massive unemployment would lead to unprecedented levels of homelessness and hunger.

Many people would leave cities looking for places to live where they could grow some food. Yet they might find all of the available land already owned by banks or the government. Without experience of farming, even those who succeeded in gaining access to acreage would fail to produce much food and would ruin large tracts of land in the process.

Eventually these problems would sort themselves out; people and social systems would adapt — but probably not before an immense human and environmental tragedy had ensued.

I wish I could say that this forecast is exaggerated for effect. Yet the actual events could be far more violent and disruptive than it is possible to suggest in so short a summary.

Examples and Strategies

Things don't have to turn out that way. As I have already said, I believe that the de-industrialization of agriculture could be carried out in a way that is not catastrophic and that in fact substantially benefits society and the environment in the long run. But to be convinced of the thesis we need more than promises — we need historic examples and proven strategies. Fortunately, we have two of each.

In some respects the most relevant example is that of Cuba's Special Period.[4] In the early 1990s, with the collapse of the Soviet Union, Cuba lost its source of cheap oil. Its industrialized agricultural system, which was heavily fuel-dependent, immediately faltered. Very quickly, Cuban leaders abandoned the Soviet industrial model of production, changing from a fuel- and petrochemical-intensive farming method to a more localized, labor-intensive, organic mode of production.

How they did this is itself an interesting story. Eco-agronomists at Cuban universities had already been advocating a transition somewhat along these lines. However, they were making little or no headway. When the crisis hit, they were given free rein to, in effect, redesign the entire Cuban food system. Had these academics not had a plan waiting in the wings, the nation's fate might have been sealed.

Heeding their advice, the Cuban government broke up large, state-owned farms and introduced private farms, farmer co-ops, and farmer markets. Cuban farmers began breeding oxen for animal traction. The Cuban people adopted a largely vegetarian diet, mostly involuntarily (meat eating went from twice a day to twice a week). They increased their intake of vegetable sources of protein and farmers reduced the growing of wheat and rice (Green Revolution crops that required too many inputs). Urban gardens (including rooftop gardens) were encouraged, and today they produce 50 to 80 percent of vegetables consumed in cities.

Early on, it was realized that more farmers were needed, and that this would require education. All of the nation's colleges and universities quickly added courses on agronomy. At the same time, wages for farmers were raised to be at parity with those for engineers and doctors. Many people moved from the cities to the country; in some cases there were incentives, in others the move was forced.

The result was survival. The average Cuban lost 20 pounds of body weight, but in the long run the overall health of the nation's people actually improved. Today, Cuba has a stable, slowly growing economy. There are few if any luxuries, but everyone has enough to eat. Having seen the benefit of smaller-scale organic production, Cuba's leaders have decided that even if they find another source of cheap oil, they will maintain a commitment to their new, decentralized, low-energy methods.

I don't want to give the impression that Cubans sailed through the Special Period unscathed. Cuba was a grim place during these years, and to this day food is far from plentiful by

Victory Gardens were a project for all age groups and involved local shows and fairs where prizes were given for the best of everything, as was the case for these school gardeners in Lincoln, Nebraska in 1944. Credit: Nebraska State Historical Society.

American standards. My point is not that Cuba is some sort of paradise, but simply that matters could have been far worse.

It could be objected that Cuba's experience holds few lessons for our own nation, since Cuba has a very different government and climate.

Let us, then, consider an indigenous historical example. During both World Wars, Americans planted Victory Gardens. During both periods, gardening became a sort of spontaneous popular movement, which (at least during World War II) the USDA initially tried to suppress, believing that it would compromise the industrialization of agriculture. It wasn't until Eleanor Roosevelt planted a Victory Garden on the White House lawn that the agriculture secretary relented; his agency then began to promote Victory Gardens and take credit for them. At the height of the movement, Victory Gardens were producing roughly 40 percent of America's vegetables, an extraordinary achievement in so short a time.[5]

By 1945, Victory Gardens were being actively promoted by the US Department of Agriculture. In the early days of World War II, the USDA tried to discourage Victory Gardens out of concern that they would inhibit the development of industrial agriculture. Credit: US Department of Agriculture

In addition to these historical precedents, we have new techniques developed with the coming agricultural crisis in mind; two of the most significant are Permaculture and Biointensive farming (there are others — such as efforts by Wes Jackson of The Land Institute to breed perennial grain crops — but limitations of time and space require me to pick and choose).

Permaculture was developed in the late 1970s by Australian ecologists Bill Mollison and David Holmgren in anticipation of exactly the problem we see unfolding before us. Holmgren defines Permaculture as "consciously designed landscapes that mimic the patterns and relationships found in nature, while yielding an abundance of food, fiber, and energy for provision of local needs."[6] Common Permaculture strategies include mulching, rainwater capture using earthworks such as swales, composting, and the harmonious integration of aquaculture, horticulture, and small-scale animal operations. A typical Permaculture farm may produce a small cash crop but it concentrates largely on self-sufficiency and soil building. Significantly, Permaculture has played an important role in Cuba's adaptation to a low-energy food regime.

Biointensive farming has been developed primarily by Californian John Jeavons, author of *How to Grow More Vegetables*. Like Permaculture, "Grow Biointensive" is a product of research begun in the 1970s. Biointensive farming has been defined as

> ... an organic agricultural system that focuses on maximum yields from the minimum area of land, while simultaneously improving the soil. The goal of the method is long-term sustainability on a closed-system basis. Because biointensive is practiced on a relatively small scale, it is well suited

Permaculture integrates domestic animals with the production of fruits and vegetables, as well as fiber and fuel crops, as on this small-scale organic farm on the Swabian Mountains in Germany. Credit: Ewig Lernender

to anything from personal or family to community gardens, market gardens, or minifarms. It has also been used successfully on small scale commercial farms.[7]

Like Holmgren and Mollison, Jeavons has worked for the past three decades in anticipation of the need to de-industrialize food production due to accumulating environmental damage and fossil fuel depletion. Currently, Biointensive farming is being taught extensively in Africa and South America as a sustainable alternative to globalized monocropping. The term "biointensive" suggests that what we are discussing here is not a de-intensification of food production, but rather the development of production along entirely different lines. While both Permaculture and Biointensive have shown themselves capable of dramatically improving yields-per-acre, their developers clearly understand that even these methods will eventually fail us unless we also limit demand for food by gradually and humanely limiting the size of the human population.

In short, it is possible in principle for industrial nations like the US to make the transition to smaller-scale, non-petroleum food production, given certain conditions. There are both precedents and models.

However, all of them imply more farmers. Here's the catch — and here's where the ancillary benefits kick in.

The Key: More Farmers!

One way or another, re-ruralization will be the dominant social trend of the 21st century. Thirty or forty years from now — again, one way or another — we will see a more historically normal ratio of rural to urban population, with the majority once again living in small, farming communities, despite current trends in the other direction. More food will be produced in cities than is the case today, but cities will be smaller. Millions more people than today will be in the countryside growing food.

They won't be doing so the way farmers do it today, and perhaps not the way farmers did it in 1900.

Indeed, we need perhaps to redefine the term *farmer*. We have

come to think of a farmer as someone with 500 acres and a big tractor and other expensive machinery. But this is not what farmers
looked like a hundred years ago, and it's not an accurate picture of
most current farmers in less-industrialized countries. Nor does it co-
incide with what will be needed in the coming decades. We should
perhaps start thinking of a farmer as someone with 3 to 50 acres,
who uses mostly hand labor and twice a year borrows a small tractor
which she or he fuels with ethanol or biodiesel produced on-site.

How many more farmers are we talking about? Currently the
US has three or four million of them, depending on how we define
the term.

Let's again consider Cuba's experience: in its transition away
from fossil-fueled agriculture, that nation found that it required 15
to 25 percent of its population to become involved in food production. In America in 1900, nearly 40 percent of the population
farmed; the current proportion is close to one percent.

Do the math for yourself. Extrapolated to this country's future
requirements, this implies the need for a minimum of 40 to 50 million additional farmers as oil and gas availability declines.

How soon will the need arise? Assuming that the peak of global
oil production occurs within the next five years, and that North
American natural gas is already in decline, we are looking at a transition that must occur over the next 20 to 30 years, and that must
begin approximately now.

Fortunately there are some hopeful trends to point to. The
stereotypical American farmer is a middle-aged, Euro-American
male, but the millions of new farmers in our future will have to include a broad mix of people, reflecting America's increasing diversity. Already the fastest growth in farm operators in America is
among female full-time farmers, as well as Hispanic, Asian, and Native American farm operators.

Another positive trend worth noting: in the Northeast US,
where the soil is acidic and giant agribusiness has not established
as much of a foothold as elsewhere, the number of small farms is
increasing. Young adults — not in the millions, but at least in the
hundreds — are aspiring to become Permaculture or organic or

Biointensive farmers. Farmers markets and community-supported agriculture farms (CSAs) are established or springing up throughout the region. This is also somewhat the case on the Pacific coast, although much less so in the Midwest and South.

What will it take to make these tentative trends the predominant ones? Among other things we will need good, helpful policies. The USDA will need to cease supporting and encouraging industrial monocropping for export, and begin supporting smaller farms, rewarding those that make the effort to reduce inputs and to grow for local consumption. In the absence of USDA policy along these lines, we need to pursue state, county, and municipal efforts to support small farms in various ways, through favorable zoning, by purchasing local food for school lunches, and so on.

We will also require land reform. Those millions of new farmers will need access to the soil, and there must be some means of making land available for this purpose. Here we might take inspiration from Indian Line Farm, a model for farmland preservation and conservation, which pioneered the use of conservation easements and community land trusts to make farmland available to working farmers.[8]

Since so few people currently know much about farming, education will be essential. Universities and community colleges have both the opportunity and responsibility to quickly develop programs in small-scale ecological farming methods — programs that also include training in other skills that farmers will need, such as marketing and formulating business plans.

Since few if any farms are financially successful the first year or even the second or third, loans and grants will also be necessary to help farmers get started.

These new farmers will need higher, stabilized food prices. But high food prices, and likely food scarcities, will pose enormous problems for consumers. As difficult as it may be to imagine now, food rationing may be required at some point in the next two or three decades. That quota system needs to be organized in such a way as to make sure everyone has the bare essentials, and to support the people at the base of the food system — the farmers.

Finally, we need a revitalization of farming communities and farming culture. A century ago, even in the absence of the air and auto transport systems we now take for granted, small towns across this land strove to provide their citizens with lectures, concerts, libraries, and yearly chautauquas. Over the past decades these same towns have seen their best and brightest young people flee first to distant colleges and then to the cities. The folks left behind have done their best to maintain a cultural environment, but in all too many cases that now consists of a movie theater and a couple of video rental stores. Farming communities must be interesting, attractive places if we expect people to inhabit them and for children to want to stay there.

If We Do This Well

We have been trained to admire the benefits of intensification and industrialization. But, as I've already indicated, we have paid an enormous price for these benefits — a price that includes alienation from nature, loss of community and tradition, and the acceptance of the anonymity and loss of autonomy implied by mass society. In essence, this tradeoff has its origins in the beginnings of urbanization and agriculture.

Could we regain much of what we have lost? Yes, perhaps by going back, at least in large part, to horticulture. Recall that the shift from horticulture to agriculture was, as best we can tell, a fateful turning point in cultural history. It represented the beginning of full-time division of labor, hierarchy, and patriarchy.

Biointensive farming and Permaculture are primarily horticultural rather than agricultural systems. These new, intelligent forms of horticulture could, then, offer an alternative to a new feudalism with a new peasantry. In addition, they emphasize biodiversity, averting many of the environmental impacts of field cropping. They use various strategies to make hand labor as efficient as possible, minimizing toil and drudgery. And they typically slash water requirements for crops grown in arid regions.

We have gotten used to a situation where most farmers rely on non-farm income. As of 2002 only a bit less than 60 percent of farm operators reported that their primary work is on the farm. Only nine percent of primary operators on farms with one operator, and ten percent on farms with multiple operators, reported all of their income as coming from the farm.

The bad side of this is that it's hard to make a living farming these days. The good side is that we don't have to think of farming as an exclusive occupation. As people return to small communities and to farming, they could bring other interests with them. Rather than a new peasantry that spends all of its time in drudgery, we could look forward to a new population of producers who maintain interests in the arts and sciences, in history, philosophy, spirituality, and psychology — in short, the whole range of pursuits than make modern urban life interesting and worthwhile.

Moreover, the re-ruralization program I am describing could be a springboard for the rebirth of democracy in this nation. Over the past few years democracy in America has become little more than a slogan. In fact this erosion of our democratic traditions has been going on for some time. As Kirkpatrick Sale showed in his wonderful book *Human Scale,* as communities grow in size, individuals' abilities to influence the affairs within them tend to shrink.[9] Sociological research now shows that people who have the ability to influence policy in their communities show a much higher sense of satisfaction with life in general.[10] In short, the re-ruralization of America could represent the fulfillment of Thomas Jefferson's vision of an agrarian democracy — but without the slaves.

If we do this well, it could mean the revitalization not only of democracy, but of the family and of authentic, place-based culture. It could also serve as the basis for a new, genuine conservatism to replace the ersatz conservatism of the current ruling political elites.

What I am proposing is nothing less than a new alliance among environmental organizations, farmers, gardeners, organizations promoting economic justice, the anti-globalization movement, universities and colleges, local businesses, churches, and other social organizations. Moreover, the efforts of this alliance would have to be coordinated at the national, state, and local level. This is clearly a tall order. However, we are not talking about merely a good idea. This is a survival strategy.

It may seem that I am describing and advocating a reversion to the world of 1800, or even that of 8000 BCE. This is not really the case. We will of course need to relearn much of what our ancestors knew. But we have discovered a great deal about biology, geology, hydrology, and other relevant subjects in recent decades, and we should be applying that knowledge — as Holmgren, Mollison, Jeavons, and others have done — to the project of producing food for ourselves.

Cultural anthropology teaches us that the way people get their food is the most reliable determinant of virtually all other social characteristics. Thus, as we build a different food system we will inevitably be building a new kind of culture, certainly very different from industrial urbanism but probably also from what preceded it. As always before in human history, we will make it up as we go along, in response to necessity and opportunity.

Perhaps these great changes won't take place until the need is obvious and irresistibly pressing. Maybe gasoline needs to get to $10 a gallon. Perhaps unemployment will have to rise to 10 or 20 or 40 percent, with families begging for food in the streets, before embattled policy makers begin to reconsider their commitment to industrial agriculture.

But even in that case, as in Cuba, all may depend upon having another option already articulated. Without that, we will be left to the worst possible outcome.

Rather than consigning ourselves to that fate, let us accept the current challenge — the next great energy transition — as an opportunity not to try vainly to preserve business as usual (the American Way of Life that, we are told, is not up for negotiation), but rather to re-imagine human culture from the ground up, using our intelligence and passion for the welfare of the next generations, and the integrity of nature's web, as our primary guides.

3

(post-) Hydrocarbon Aesthetics

T HOUGH I COULD HARDLY call myself a professional violin-
ist these days, I still get the occasional call for a wedding or
other special function, and I cherish these increasingly rare opportunities to work alongside competent players. This past April I was
hired to play in a string quartet to provide the requisite "musical
wallpaper" for the opening of a traveling exhibit ("International
Arts and Crafts: From William Morris to Frank Lloyd Wright") at
the de Young Museum in San Francisco. As a gratuity to the musicians, the Museum offered us each a pair of tickets to the exhibit.
Since my wife Janet and I have long been fascinated by the Arts and
Crafts movement, we used our tickets a few weeks later.

The exhibit included top examples of the British, German,
Scandinavian, American, and Japanese versions of the genre. There
were fabric and book designs by William Morris, interiors by Frank
Lloyd Wright, and furnishings by C.F.A. Yoysey and others.

As Janet and I walked through the exhibition I couldn't help but
reflect on its implications for humanity's aesthetic past, present, and
future.

The Arts and Crafts movement was, in essence, a critical response to the industrial revolution. William Morris, the movement's
founder, saw the industrialization of Britain and deplored the results. Farmers, craftspeople, and manual workers often could not
compete economically with fuel-fed engines, and so vocations and

William Morris. Credit: Public Domain

William Morris designed type fonts and translated medieval and classical texts, but he was especially famed for his fabrics and wallpaper. Credit: Public Domain

skills that had developed over generations vanished in favor of jobs tending machines. But of course it was impossible for the machines to work intelligently or soulfully as humans do, and so the aesthetic environment of Britain became progressively more denatured and dehumanized.

During Morris's lifetime, the usual designs of mass production merely imitated the symbolic elements of architecture and furnishings from previous eras. As the burgeoning middle class sought outer reassurance of its attainments, the factory system obliged with the ornate facades and kitsch bric-a-brac fashioned to impart an upper-class aura. Victorian buildings and cluttered parlors displayed an incoherent regurgitation of Greek, Roman, Renaissance, Egyptian, Chinese, and occasionally Aztec or Mayan themes mixed and mutilated often beyond recognition.

Morris and his colleagues drew inspiration instead from the philosophy of John Ruskin, especially as set forth in the books *The Stones of Venice* and *Unto this Last,* which related the moral and social health of a nation to the qualities of its architecture and designs. For Ruskin, and subsequently for Morris and other followers of the movement, the spirit of industrialism began with the Renaissance, when the rising mercantile class devalued and destroyed the traditions of free and mostly anonymous artists and craftspeople who had worked independently throughout the medieval period to build the free cities and great cathedrals of Europe.

Already, by the 16th century, architects, builders, painters, and carpenters had become mere hired workers whose efforts were mostly directed by — and meant to glorify — wealthy burghers. Thus, for Ruskin and Morris, inspiration had to come from an earlier era — the Gothic period, in which (in Morris's words) "guildsmen of the Free Cities" enjoyed a "freedom of the hand and mind subordinated to the collective harmony which made freedom possible." Morris's aesthetic was thus politically grounded, and he, together with socialist colleagues like Walter Crane and Charles Robert Ashbee, looked not only backward in history but also forward — to an attainable, simpler way of life in which craftspeople, working in guilds, would control their own lives as well as the economies of cities and nations.

The aesthetic sensibilities of Morris and his followers echoed those of the Pre-Raphaelite painters such as Edward Burne-Jones, who were similarly inspired by Ruskin's *The Stones of Venice*, and especially by the chapter "The Nature of Gothic." Both movements sought to promote a practical alternative to the domination of humanity by its tools — and implicitly, by the enormous energies unleashed from fossil fuels.

The Arts and Crafts artisans

Louis Welden Hawkins's "Fächer auf goldenem Grund" exemplifies the spirit of Symbolism and Art Nouveau — stylized, flowing, curvilinear, and usually based on vegetal motifs. Credit: DIRECTMEDIA Publishing

Frank Lloyd Wright. Credit: Public Domain

aimed at a quality of design characterized by an organic simplicity that flowed from honoring both the raw materials and the skill of the individual worker. Decorative themes emerged from functional necessity and from regional vernacular design vocabularies.

Art Nouveau was the Arts and Crafts movement's decadent cousin. It produced luscious tendril-limned furniture and facades, but lacked the earnest social philosophy of Morris and his disciples.

In North America, Frank Lloyd Wright led the "prairie school" of architecture, which sought to make buildings fit into the landscape rather than arbitrarily dominate it. Wright hated the modern industrial city and its ubiquitous symbol, the skyscraper, which he regarded as a "human filing cabinet." "The skyscraper as the typical expression of the city," he wrote, "is the human stable, stalls filled with the herd, all to be milked by the system that keeps the animals docile by such fodder as it puts in the manger and such warmth as the crowd instills in the crowd."[1] Wright viewed the urban street grid and the skyscraper as mere expedients of power and social control with "no higher ideal than commercial success." A truly democratic society, he argued, must consist of a decentralized, organic human community integrated into the landscape around it.

Another American proponent of the Arts and Crafts sensibility was Elbert Hubbard of East Aurora, New York, who headed a community of artisans known as the Roycrofters. Hubbard was a home-spun Yankee craftsman-philosopher, the kind of self-taught natural leader who, if he had lived in the 1970s, would probably have been the guru of a hippie cult. A congenital aphorist with vaguely right-wing political views (his most famous writing was the astonishingly popular pamphlet, "A Message to Garcia," which extolled the dili-

Frank Lloyd Wright's Fallingwater House. Wright sought to make his build-ings a part of the landscape; this, the only one of his houses now open to the public, particularly exemplifies his concept of an organic architecture that promotes harmony between humans and nature through design. As was his typical practice, Wright designed all of the furnishings as well. Credit: GNU/Creative Commons

gence of a soldier in the Spanish American war who helped turn Cuba into a *de facto* US colony), Hubbard preached independence and hard work but seldom criticized the expanding corporate struc-tures of the American economy that were systematically undermin-ing the livelihoods of small farmers and artisans. When Hubbard perished on the Lusitania in 1914, the Roycrofters lost their spokes-man and guiding light. They soldiered on for a few years, but by the end of the '20s were merely reproducing a few popular designs from their heyday of making original lamps, bookends, vases, chairs, and tables. Today in East Aurora one can still visit some of the Roy-crofters' old workshops and savor the afterglow of their happy ex-periment.

The Arts and Crafts movement also spread to continental Europe and Japan, in each instance acquiring the local flavors not only of traditional design elements but of indigenous social philoso-phies.

Nevertheless, by the end of the 1920s, the movement had mostly disappeared. Sadly but predictably, Morris and his followers had failed to create an enduring artisanal paradise. Industrialism and capitalism swallowed and digested their efforts, which in the end merely yielded buildings and ornaments for middle- and upper-class consumption.

Designing for the Tragic Interlude of Cheap Abundance

By the late 1920s the industrial megamachine was extruding heaps of new objects with no Gothic predecessors. The most obvious and commercially significant was the personal automobile (what would a Gothic motorcar look like? — surely nothing like the faux-Gothic hotrod on the old *Munsters* TV show). Here was the Machine Triumphant, the symbol and substance of personal attainment and ease of movement. Another significant invention was the airplane, with its capability of transcending limits of space and time through vertical ascent and sheer speed. As aircraft designers gradually began to appreciate the functional benefits of aerodynamics, the *look* of the airplane (and, for a while, that of the dirigible) began to be appropriated for use on objects whose function had little or nothing to do with flight or rapid motion — from staplers and blenders to lamps and toasters.

This transition from over-wrought Victorianism to streamlined modernism came about during a period when, with so many new inventions needing a marketable "look," industrial design emerged as a burgeoning new field of specialization within the arts. Car designers competed to make fenders more voluptuous, dashboards more commanding — and to make cars look more like airplanes. Designers consciously incorporated modern style elements to stimulate sales; as advertising executive Earnest Elmo Calkins put it in a magazine article in 1927, "this new influence on articles of barter and sale is largely used to make people dissatisfied with what they have of the old order, still good and useful and efficient, but lacking in the newest touch. In the expressive slang of the day...[these goods] 'date.'"[2]

Streamlining led to an emphasis on smooth curving surfaces, long lines, and the illusion of speed. It hid the angular electrical

motors or combustion engines of machines beneath flowing metal-
lic skins, just as rumbling machines themselves cloaked the real
source of their power — fossil fuels dug from mines or drawn from
deep wells.

Streamlining was the "Look of the Future." But in retrospect,
once it had itself become "dated" by the endless imperative to rein-
vent style for the sake of sales, it became known as Art Deco.

In contrast to the Arts and Crafts style-philosophy, Art Deco
took for granted — even glorified — the machine and machine-
based production. Nevertheless, its best practitioners sought to
develop a design vocabulary (using geometry and the primitive
elements commandeered by modern artists like Picasso) that fed
the human hunger for beauty while meeting the needs of the factory and ad agency.

Many of the early pioneers of industrial design described their
efforts in idealistic terms. Architect Peter Behrens, hired in 1907 by
the German industrial firm AEG to create a unified look for the
company's products and advertising, sought to infuse his work with
a "spiritual" content as he replaced useless and tasteless ornamenta-
tion with clean, geometric lines. Here was a design philosophy for a
new age of universal freedom and convenience!

However, modern industrial design grew up alongside advertising and the increasing need for advertising. As Morris had seen and
predicted, fuel-fed machines could not help but overwhelm the
human community and the skill and pride of craftsmanship. They
likewise overwhelmed the capacity of ordinary humans to buy and
use material goods. So many goods could be produced, and so
quickly, that markets were easily saturated; hence the need on the
part of manufacturers for new, quickly expanding credit and advertising industries. More invention required more investment, which
required more capital accumulation, which in turn required more
sales — more consumption. Therefore consumption *had* to be stim-
ulated, and advertisers, using the scientific discoveries of the new
science of psychology, were eager to oblige.

Meanwhile the corporation provided the legal, economic, and
social nexus for organizing all of these efforts at finance, production,

and advertising. Itself a kind of machine, with capital its fuel, the corporation has an inbuilt imperative for growth and the accumulation of power, one that transcends the personality or ethical views of any particular manager or executive.

Industrial design provided the soul and self-image for otherwise faceless corporate power, as each corporation sought its own identifiable "personality" expressed in the color, shape, tone, and texture of its products. The result: during the 20th century, even the noblest efforts of industrial designers yielded products that were expressions of a system whose overall characteristics were dictated by scale, speed, accumulation, and efficiency—dictates that made both the shapers and ultimate users of products mere instruments for the attainment of a purpose ultimately at odds with cultural integrity, human sanity, and species survival. As Stuart Ewen put it in his brilliant book, *All Consuming Images: On the Politics of Style in Contemporary Culture:*

> In the carefully calculated design of many consumer goods, the technological supremacy of the corporation is made seemingly accessible to the consumer. While at work many people spend their lives performing routine and minuscule elements within an impenetrable bureaucratic or productive maze, the designer of many products — particularly appliances and other electronic items — suggests that with the purchase of the product, *you will have your hands on the controls.* In a world where a genuine sense of mastery is elusive, and feelings of impotency abound, the well-designed product can provide a symbolism of autonomous proficiency and power.[3]

As industrial design progressed after World War II and into the '50s, '60s, '70s, '80s, and '90s, style continued to evolve, as it had to in order to serve the purposes of fashion and planned obsolescence. Images and objects became more frankly seductive and more directly suggestive of the very qualities of which the lives of human beings were in fact being systematically drained — autonomy and creativity.

In hindsight, it appears that Deco was the last hiccup of design originality for the hydrocarbon age. Everything after it has been essentially imitative recycling. Today, the unified vision of Deco is attractively "retro," and in its place contemporary designers have managed to achieve a kind of new Victorianism consisting of a mangled, chaotically tumbled style hurled together from the detritus of the past, a style they proudly term "post-modern."

Hydrocarbon Style: Big, Fast, and Ugly

I often feel a jarring visceral response upon leaving the best museum exhibits and returning to contemporary urban existence: everything outside looks ugly and pitiful by comparison. I get the same feeling when leaving a city like Venice or Kyoto and flying back to California. It's a response I can only call aesthetic shock.

If William Morris and his followers were alive today, they might regard a stroll through a Wal-Mart as a veritable descent into hell. Yet many Americans evidently think of it as a visit to consumer paradise. Perhaps this is some gauge of the degree of our collective aesthetic degeneration.

Now, San Francisco is not the most beautiful of the world's cities, but neither is it the ugliest by a long shot (I'll spare you my nominations for that prize). Nevertheless, the endless concrete pavement, the buildings, and, more than anything else, the automobiles that surround us in most modern cities (certainly including San Francisco) are beyond dreary. The cars are so much a part of our lives that we are inured to their dominating, ubiquitous physical presence. Only when one has lived for at least a few days in an environment free from them is one likely to notice how deeply the industrial aesthetic environment is entwined with cars.

Our constant, habitual, unconscious psychic adaptation to the soullessness of the manufactured environment is part of our personal price of admission to the industrial fiesta. Who can be aesthetically proud of a car, a computer, or a refrigerator? One might be proud of *having* one, if that is in question (I am certain there are millions of new car owners in China and Russia who do feel considerable pride in this regard). But what of the object itself as a product of human artistry? Inherent in our appreciation of its design is our knowledge that the appliance in question will be used up in a decade and obsolete in half that time. Consequently, it must exhibit only as much beauty or craftsmanship as is necessary to get it off the showroom floor and into our home or garage. We are satisfied for now — but not for long.

This state of affairs might be barely acceptable if such objects were the exceptions, if we were surrounded by others that were more durable and that showed more signs of care and that nourished us in deeper ways. But in most modern industrial countries that is not the case. Our houses, our packaging, our furnishings, our electronic gadgets — all share the same disposable ephemerality-by-design. This is truly a throwaway culture. Yes, it is possible to obtain antiques (for example, I like to use old fountain pens instead of disposable plastic ballpoints), or unique art pieces, or handmade shoes, but these are anomalies and affectations. Only the wealthy can afford to surround themselves with such things. The masses instead make do with stamped-out plastic or metal objects that evince no sign whatever that any living, breathing human ever worked them or thought much about them.

As a way of concealing or compensating for this we seek out "designer" lines of merchandise with names like Calvin Klein or Martha Stewart on their labels. But these are goods whose *actual* designers are people we've never heard of, let alone ever see. One can even find faux remakes of Arts and Crafts ("Mission-style") pieces in the furniture section of Wal-Mart. What's the problem? They look just like the real thing.

As for the working conditions of the people who actually produce these objects — well, you don't know and you don't *want* to know. It doesn't take much imagining to divine what Morris would think of the situation.

Oh, To Be Hip Again

The Arts and Crafts movement inhabited the lower upside of history's energy bell-curve; now, after a century of cheap petroleum, we are just over the crest, contemplating our way back down. What happened in between was a brief, probably inevitable, but nonetheless tragic eruption of production and consumption on a scale never seen before, and never to be seen again. It is tempting to look back now, as we contemplate the downside of the curve, and view with nostalgia the ideas and productions of Morris, Wright, etc., just as they looked back to the crafts guilds of the Middle Ages.

But what will the human-made world look like a few decades beyond Peak Oil? Will we see a fulfillment of the Arts and Crafts ideal? It would be nice to think so. However, the world in which Morris and his colleagues lived and worked — including the cultural symbols, the skills, even in some cases the raw materials then readily available — has evaporated, replaced by one in which most people are loyal not to land and place, but to product and image.

One relatively recent iteration of style — the hippie aesthetic of macramé, tie-dye, beads, sandals, long hair, dulcimers, and herb gardens — may hold a few cues and clues for the post-carbon future. Hippie houses and ornaments were handmade, but often rather ineptly so. This in itself is perhaps a sign of what is to come, as we return by necessity to handcraft but without skill or cultural memory to guide us.

In its lucid moments, the hippie aesthetic (which was on the whole more musical than visual) articulated a coherent rejection of consumerism and an embrace of the "natural." But while it attempted a profound critique of the industrial-corporate system, it showed only limited similarity to Arts and Crafts ideals. This was partly because of the changed infrastructural context: by this point in history, cars and electronic machines were so embedded in the lives of people in industrialized nations that few could imagine a realistic alternative. Moreover, the baby boomers' rebellion was at least partly enabled by the very wealth that abundant energy produced: rents were cheap, transportation was cheap, and food was cheap; as a result, dropping out of the employment rat race for a few months in order to tune in and turn on carried little real personal risk. Thus their rejection and critique were inherently self-limiting.

The counterculture expressed itself through dreams of foot-loose, motored mobility (*Easy Rider*), and in music amped to the max with inexpensive electricity. The latter was hardly incidental: the voltage that made Harrison's and Clapton's guitars gently weep, and that wafted Grace Slick's and Janis Joplin's voices past the back rows in amphitheaters seating thousands — in short, the power of the music that united a generation — flowed ultimately from coal-fired generating plants. That same 110 volt, 60 cycle AC current energized stereo sets in dorm rooms and apartments across America, allowing ten million teenagers to memorize the lyrics to songs impressed on vinyl (i.e., petroleum) disks in the certain knowledge that these were revelatory words that would change the course of history.

If the hippie aesthetic was at least occasionally endearing, it was easily stereotyped and, when profitable, readily co-opted by cynical ad executives. It was also often naively uncritical of its own assumptions. If you want to appreciate for yourself the embedded contradictions of the movement, just rent and watch the movie *Woodstock*. The wide-eyed, self-congratulatory idealism of the "kids" — who arrived by automobile to liberate themselves through amateur psychopharmacology and to worship at the altar of electric amplification — is simultaneously touching and unbearable. It was no wonder the revolution failed: without an understanding of the energetic basis of industrialism and therefore of the modern corporate state, their rebellion could never have been more than symbolic.

Where the hippie aesthetic drew on deeper philosophical and political roots (such as the back-to-the-land philosophy of Scott and Helen Nearing), it persisted, as it still does to this day. Perhaps the most durable and intelligent product of the era was the design philosophy known as Permaculture, developed in Australia by ecologists Bill Mollison and David Holmgren. A practical — rather than an aesthetic — design system for producing food, energy, and shelter, Permaculture was conceived in prescient expectation of the looming era of limits, and it is endlessly adaptable to differing climates and cultures. In the future, its principles may serve as the fundamental frame of reference for builders and craftspeople as they elaborate new aesthetic styles.

Manifesto for a Post-Carbon Aesthetic

Will industrial production survive in the post-hydrocarbon era? The answer will of course depend on how much energy humans will have at their disposal. The total amount, as well as the per capita amount, will certainly be substantially reduced, especially in what are currently the most highly industrialized societies — but by how much? The very earliest factories were powered by water and wind, resources that presumably will still be available to future generations. Will these sources provide enough power to run the machine tools to make the lathes to make the sophisticated wind turbines (and other energy production devices) that will be needed in order to maintain some semblance of an electrical grid, or a manufacturing economy? It is impossible to know the answer at this point.

What can be said with confidence is that everything in the post-hydrocarbon world will operate on a smaller scale (let us hope that E. F. Schumacher was right in insisting that "small is *beautiful*"). There will be less of nearly everything to go around, and virtually every process of production and transport will occur more slowly.

The prospect of returning to human muscles for productive power is both exciting and scary. Will this mean an explosion of craftsmanship, or a return to drudgery (particularly for women)? Most likely, it will result in both. However, if adopted widely, the Permaculture design system could at least minimize the drudgery and hence provide opportunity to devote more attention to the quality and beauty of products.

At first thought, aesthetics might seem utterly incidental, given the survival challenges imposed by Peak Oil, climate chaos, mass extinctions, and so on. However, art is part of the necessary process of cultural adaptation. People inevitably find ways not just to endure, but to enjoy — to find happiness in the midst of change. We are, after all, environment shapers. As birds build nests, we build campsites, fashion clothing, and (if we are civilized humans) build cities. But as we shape our environments, those environments in turn mold our perceptions, our judgments, our expectations, our very consciousness. Art, religion, politics, and economics will all have to adjust as the world's energy infrastructure shifts. And the forms we create to express and embody those shifts and adjustments will in turn alter us. Cultural change is a process of reverberation.

It may be presumptuous to try to forecast what post-hydrocarbon style will look like, as people will have to make it up as they go along — and creativity is, almost by definition, difficult to predict. It will, by necessity, be true post-modernism — though the use of the term may be more confusing than helpful. In any case, the following are a few of the characteristics that must inevitably be part of the new aesthetic.

1. Workers will incorporate *no or minimal fossil fuels*, either as raw material or as energy source, in production processes. This is the defining condition for all that follows, and its implications will be profound.
2. Construction of buildings and objects will depend substantially on the application of *muscle power and handcraft*. This necessarily follows from (1).
3. *Pride in workmanship* will therefore return.
4. Previously cheap petrochemical-based materials (such as plastics) will gradually disappear, necessitating the use of natural materials; however, many of the latter (such as wood) will also become more rare and expensive (as is already happening). Thus workers will inevitably develop more *respect for natural materials*.
5. Because buildings and objects being produced will require more hand labor and scarce raw materials, the throwaway mentality and the phenomenon of planned obsolescence will disappear. *Durability* will be a required attribute of all products.
6. For the same reasons, *reparability* will also be requisite: the average person will need to be able to fix anything that breaks.
7. Since products themselves will need to be durable and reparable, continued rapid changes of fashion and style will seem nonsensical and counterproductive. Planned aesthetic obsolescence will be replaced by the imperative to lend an enduring *artistic quality* to all design.

8. Because the transitional era (i.e., the coming century) will be one in which species will continue to vanish, and because people will no longer be insulated from weather and other natural conditions by high-energy buildings and machines, workers will probably be inspired to incorporate *themes from nature* into their products.

9. In their efforts to identify aesthetic themes appropriate to hand labor and natural materials, workers will likely end up drawing upon *vernacular design traditions*.

10. Because people living in the transitional era will be witnessing the passing of the fossil-fueled machine culture of their youth, they will probably be inspired to incorporate occasional *ironic or nostalgic comments* on that passing into their artistic output.

11. Beauty may to a certain extent be in the eye of the beholder, but there are *universal principles of harmony and proportion* that perennially reappear. Given that workers will be required to invent much of their aesthetic vocabulary from scratch, they will no doubt fall back on these principles frequently.

12. Since we are entering an era of declining availability of raw materials, the new aesthetic will by necessity emphasize *leanness and simplicity*, and will eschew superfluous decoration. The Zen architecture of Japan may serve as an inspiration in this regard.

These are, of course, only the most general of parameters within which specific new regional styles may emerge over the coming decades. What exactly these styles will look like won't be known until millions of craftspeople and builders undertake the processes of (re-)learning skills and producing large numbers of buildings, tools, furnishings, and artworks. However, one can hardly help noting that most of the characteristics listed above apply to the products of the Arts and Crafts movement.

Perhaps the way down the hydrocarbon curve will, at least in the best instances, indeed look a little like the way up.

On Nature's Limits
and the Human Condition

4

Five Axioms of Sustainability

M Y AIM IN THIS CHAPTER is to explore the history of the terms *sustainable* and *sustainability,* and their various published definitions, and then to offer a set of five axioms (based on a review of the literature) to help clarify the characteristics of a durable society.

The essence of the term *sustainable* is simple enough: "that which can be maintained over time." By implication, this means that any society, or any aspect of a society, that is unsustainable cannot be maintained for long and will cease to function at some point.

It is probably safe to assume that no society can be maintained forever: astronomers assure us that in several billion years the sun will heat to the point that Earth's oceans will boil away and life on our planet will come to an end. Thus *sustainability* is a relative term. It seems reasonable to take as a temporal frame of reference the durations of prior civilizations, which ranged from several hundred to several thousand years. A sustainable society, then, would be one capable of maintaining itself for many centuries into the future.

However, the word *sustainable* has become widely used in recent years to refer, in a general and vague way, to practices that are reputed to be more environmentally sound than others. Often the word is used so carelessly as to lead some environmentalists to advise abandoning its use.[1] Nevertheless, I believe that the concept of sustainability is essential to understanding and solving our species' ecological dilemma, and that the word is capable of rehabilitation, if only we are willing to expend a little effort in arriving at a clear definition.

History and Background

The essential concept of sustainability was embodied in the world-views and traditions of many indigenous peoples; for example, it was a precept of the *Gayanashagowa,* or Great Law of Peace (the constitution of the Haudenosaunee or Six Nations of the Iroquois Confederacy) that chiefs consider the impact of their decisions on the seventh generation to come.

The first known European use of *sustainability* (German: *Nach-haltigkeit)* occurred in 1712 in the book *Sylvicultura Oeconomica* by German forester and scientist Hanns Carl von Carlowitz. Later, French and English foresters adopted the practice of planting trees as a path to "sustained yield forestry."

The term gained widespread usage after 1987, when the Brundt-land Report of the World Commission on Environment and Development defined *sustainable development* as development that "meets the needs of the present generation without compromising the ability of future generations to meet their own needs."[2] This definition of sustainability has proven extremely influential, and is still widely used; nevertheless, it has been criticized for its failure to explicitly note the unsustainability of the use of non-renewable resources, and for its general disregard of the problem of population growth.[3]

Also in the 1980s, Swedish oncologist Dr. Karl-Henrik Robèrt brought together leading Swedish scientists to develop a consensus on requirements for a sustainable society. In 1989 he formulated this consensus in four conditions for sustainability, which in turn became the basis for an organization, The Natural Step.[4] Subsequently, 60 major Swedish corporations and 56 municipalities, as well as many businesses in other nations, pledged to abide by Natural Step conditions. The four conditions are as follows:

1. In order for a society to be sustainable, nature's functions and diversity are not systematically subject to increasing concentrations of substances extracted from the earth's crust.

2. In order for a society to be sustainable, nature's functions and diversity are not systematically subject to increasing concentrations of substances produced by society.

3. In order for a society to be sustainable, nature's functions and diversity are not systematically impoverished by physical displacement, over-harvesting, or other forms of ecosystem manipulation.

4. In a sustainable society, people are not subject to conditions that systematically undermine their capacity to meet their needs.

Seeing the need for an accounting or indicator scheme by which to measure sustainability, in 1992 Canadian ecologist William Rees introduced the concept of the ecological footprint, defined as the amount of land and water area a human population would hypothetically need in order to provide the resources required to support itself and to absorb its wastes, given prevailing technology.[5] Implicit in the scheme is the recognition that, for humanity to achieve sustainability, the total world population's footprint must be less than the total land/water area of the Earth. That footprint is currently calculated by the Footprint Network as being about 23 percent larger than what the planet can regenerate, indicating that humankind is to this extent operating in an unsustainable manner.

In a paper published in 1994 (and revised in 1998), physics professor Albert A. Bartlett offered 17 Laws of Sustainability, with which he sought to clarify the meaning of *sustainability* in terms of population and resource consumption.[6] Bartlett's criticisms of the careless use of the term, and his rigorous demonstration of the implications of continued growth, were important influences on the present author's efforts to define what is genuinely sustainable.

A truly comprehensive historical survey of the usage of the terms *sustainable* and *sustainability* is not feasible. A search of Amazon.com for *sustainability* (January 17, 2007) yielded nearly 25,000 hits — presumably indicating several thousand distinct titles containing the word. *Sustainable* yielded 62,000 hits, including books on sustainable leadership, communities, energy, design, construction, business, development, urban planning, tourism, and so on. A search of journal articles on Google Scholar turned up 538,000 hits, indicating thousands of scholarly articles or references with the word *sustainability* in their titles. However, my own admittedly less-than-exhaustive acquaintance with the literature (informed, among other sources, by two books that offer an overview of the history of the concept of sustainability)[7] suggests that much, if not most of this immense body of publications repeats, or is based on, the definitions and conditions described above.

Five Axioms

As a contribution to this ongoing refinement of the concept, I have formulated five axioms (self-evident truths) of sustainability. I have not introduced any fundamentally new notions in any of the axioms; my goal is simply to distill ideas that have been proposed and explored by others, and to put them into a form that is both more precise and easier to understand.

In formulating these axioms I endeavored to take into account previous definitions of sustainability, and also the most cogent criticisms of those definitions. My criteria were as follows:

- To qualify as an axiom, a statement must be capable of being tested using the methodology of science.
- Collectively, a set of axioms intended to define sustainability must be minimal (with no redundancies).
- At the same time, the axioms must be sufficient, leaving no glaring loopholes.
- The axioms should be worded in terms the layperson can understand.

Here are the axioms, each followed by a brief discussion:

1. Tainter's Axiom: Any society that continues to use critical resources unsustainably will collapse.
Exception: A society can avoid collapse by finding replacement resources.
Limit to the exception: **In a finite world, the number of possible replacements is also finite.**

I have named this axiom for Joseph Tainter, author of the classic study, *The Collapse of Complex Societies,* which demonstrates that collapse is a frequent if not universal fate of complex societies. He argues that collapse is directly related to declining returns on efforts to support growing levels of societal complexity with energy harvested from the environment. Jared Diamond's book *Collapse: How Societies Choose to Fail or Succeed* similarly makes the argument that collapse is the common destiny of societies that ignore resource constraints.[8]

This axiom defines sustainability by the consequences of its absence, i.e., collapse. Tainter defines *collapse* as a reduction in social complexity — i.e., a contraction of society in terms of its population size, the sophistication of its technologies, the consumption rates of its people, and the diversity of its specialized social roles. Often, historically, collapse has meant a precipitous decline in population brought about by social chaos, warfare, disease, or famine. However, collapse can also occur more gradually over a period of many decades or even several centuries. There is also the theoretical possibility that a society could choose to "collapse" (i.e., reduce its complexity) in a controlled as well as gradual manner.

While it could be argued that a society can choose to change rather than collapse, the only choices that would prevent collapse would be either to cease using critical resources unsustainably or to find alternative resources.

A society that uses resources sustainably may collapse for other reasons, some beyond the society's control (an overwhelming natural disaster, or conquest by another, more militarily formidable and aggressive society, to name just two of many possibilities), so it cannot be said that a sustainable society is immune to collapse unless many more conditions for sustainability are specified than in this axiom. This first axiom focuses on resource consumption because that is a decisive, quantifiable, and, in principle, controllable determinant of a society's long-term survival.

The question of what constitutes sustainable or unsustainable use of resources is addressed in Axioms 3 and 4.

Critical resources are those essential to the maintenance of life and basic social functions, including (but not necessarily limited to) water and the means and materials necessary to produce food and usable energy.

The *exception* and *limit to the exception* address the common argument of free-market economists that resources are infinitely substitutable, and that therefore modern market-driven societies need never face a depletion-led collapse, even if their consumption rates continue to escalate.[9] In some instances, substitutes for resources do become readily available and are even superior, as was the case in the mid-19th century when kerosene from petroleum was substituted for whale oil as a fuel for lamps. In other cases, substitutes are inferior, as is the case with tar sands as a substitute for conventional petroleum, given that tar sands are less energy-dense, require more energy input for processing, and produce more carbon emissions. As time goes on, societies will tend first to exhaust substitutes that are superior and easy to get at, then those that are equivalent, and increasingly will have to rely on ever more inferior substitutes to replace depleting resources — unless rates of consumption are held in check (see Axioms 2–4).

2. Bartlett's Axiom: Population growth and/or growth in the rates of consumption of resources cannot be sustained.

I have named this axiom for Albert A. Bartlett because it is his First Law of Sustainability, reproduced verbatim (I found it impossible to improve upon).[10]

The world has seen the human population grow for many decades and therefore this growth has obviously been sustained up to the present. How can we be sure that it cannot be sustained into the indefinite future? Simple arithmetic shows that even small rates of growth, if continued, add up to absurdly large — and plainly unsupportable — population sizes and rates of consumption. For example, a simple one percent rate of growth in the present human population (less than the actual current rate) would result in a doubling of population each 70 years. Thus in 2075, the Earth would be home to 13 billion humans; in 2145, 26 billion; and so on. By the year 3050, there would be one human per square meter of the Earth's land surface (including mountains and deserts).

Essentially the same thing is true with regards to consumption. Just one example: there are 330 million cubic miles of water on Earth and, while it is difficult to say just how much of that humans use annually (because many uses, such as fishing, are indirect), it would probably be fair to estimate that we use one million cubic miles. Let us assume that future humans will find a way to make all of the Earth's water usable, that human population stays as it is, but that per capita use of water grows one percent annually. By the year 2600 humans would be using every drop of water on the planet.

3. To be sustainable, the use of *renewable* resources must proceed at a rate that is less than or equal to the rate of natural replenishment.

Renewable resources are exhaustible. Forests can be over-cut, resulting in barren landscapes and shortages of wood (as occurred in many parts of Europe in past centuries), and fish can be over-harvested, resulting in the extinction or near-extinction of many species (as is occurring today globally).

This axiom has been stated, in somewhat differing ways, by many economists and ecologists, and is the basis for "sustained yield forestry" (see above) and "maximum sustainable yield" fishery management. Efforts to refine this essential principle of sustainability are ongoing.[11]

The term "rate of natural replenishment" requires some discussion. The first clue that harvesting is proceeding at a rate greater than that of natural replenishment is the decline of the resource base. However, a resource may be declining for reasons other than over-harvesting; for example, a forest that is not being logged may be decimated by disease. Nevertheless, if the resource is declining, pursuit of the goal of sustainability requires that the rate of harvest be reduced, regardless of the cause. Sometimes harvests must drop dramatically, at a rate far greater than the rate of resource decline, so that the resource has time to recover. This has been the case with regard to whale and fish species that have been overharvested to the point of near exhaustion, and have required complete harvest moratoria in order to re-establish themselves — though in cases where the remaining breeding population is too small even this is not enough and the species cannot recover.

Axiom 3 is implied in the Natural Step's third condition.

*4. To be sustainable, the use of **non-renewable** resources must proceed at a rate that is declining, and the **rate of decline** must be greater than or equal to the **rate of depletion**.*

*(The **rate of depletion** is defined as the amount being extracted and used during a specified time interval, usually a year, as a percentage of the amount left to extract.)*

No continuous rate of use of any non-renewable resource is sustainable. However, if the rate of use is declining at a rate greater than or equal to the rate of depletion, this can be said to be a sustainable situation in that society's dependence on the resource will be reduced to insignificance before the resource is exhausted.

This principle was first stated, in a more generalized and more mathematically rigorous form, by Albert A. Bartlett in his 1986 paper, "Sustained Availability: A Management Program for Non-Renewable Resources."[12] The article's abstract notes:

> If the rate of extraction declines at a fixed fraction per unit time, the rate of extraction will approach zero, but the integrated total of the extracted resource between t=0 and t=infinity will remain finite. If we choose a rate of decline of the rate of extraction of the resource such that the integrated total of all future extraction equals the present size of the remaining resource then we have a program that will allow the resource to be available in declining amounts for use forever.

Annually reducing the rate of extraction of a given non-renewable resource by its yearly rate of depletion effectively accomplishes the same thing, but requires only simple arithmetic and layperson's terms for its explanation.

Estimates of the "amount left to extract," mentioned in the axiom, are disputable for all non-renewable resources. Unrealistically robust estimates would tend to skew the depletion rate in a downward direction, undermining any effort to attain sustainability via a resource depletion protocol. It may be realistic to assume that people in the future will find ways to extract non-renewable resources more thoroughly, with amounts that would otherwise be left in the ground becoming economically recoverable as a result of higher commodity prices and improvements in extraction technology. Also, exploration techniques are likely to improve, leading to further discoveries of the resource. Thus realistic estimates of ultimately recoverable quantities should be greater than currently known amounts extractable with current technology at current prices. However, it is unrealistic to assume that people in the future will ever be able to economically extract all of a given resource, or that limits of declining marginal returns in the extraction process will no longer apply. Moreover, if discovery rates are currently declining, it is probably unrealistic to assume that they will increase substantially in the future. Thus for any non-renewable resource prudence dictates adhering to conservative estimates of the "amount left to extract."

Axiom 4 encapsulates Bartlett's 7th and 8th Laws of Sustainability. It is also the basis for the Oil Depletion Protocol, first suggested by petroleum geologist Colin J. Campbell in 1996 and the subject of a recent book by the present author.[13] The aim of the Oil Depletion Protocol is to reduce global consumption of petroleum in order to avert the crises likely to ensue as a result of declining supply — including economic collapse and resource wars. Under the terms of the Oil Depletion Protocol, oil-importing countries would reduce their imports by the world oil depletion rate (calculated by Campbell at 2.5 percent per year); producers would reduce their domestic production by their national depletion rates.

5. Sustainability requires that substances introduced into the environment from human activities be minimized and rendered harmless to biosphere functions.

In cases where pollution from the extraction and consumption of non-renewable resources that have proceeded at expanding rates for some time threatens the viability of ecosystems, reduction in the rates of extraction and consumption of those resources may need to occur at a rate greater than the rate of depletion.

If Axioms 2 through 4 are followed, pollution should be minimized as a result. Nevertheless, these conditions are not sufficient in all cases to avert potentially collapse-inducing impacts.

It is possible for a society to generate serious pollution from the unwise use of renewable resources (the use of tanning agents on hides damaged streams for centuries or millennia), and such impacts are to be avoided. Likewise, especially where large numbers of humans are concentrated, their biological wastes may pose severe environmental problems. Such wastes must be properly composted.

The most serious forms of pollution in the modern world arise from the extraction, processing, and consumption of non-renewable resources. If (as outlined in Axiom 4) the consumption of non-renewable resources declines, pollution should also decline. However, in the current instance, where the extraction and consumption of non-renewable resources have been growing for some time and have resulted in levels of pollution that threaten basic biosphere functions, heroic measures are called for. This is, of course, the situation with regard to atmospheric concentrations of greenhouse gases, especially in relation to the burning of coal, a non-renewable resource; it is also the case with regard to hormone-mimicking petrochemical pollution that inhibits reproduction in many vertebrate species. Merely to reduce coal consumption by the global coal depletion rate will not suffice to avert a climatic catastrophe. The coal depletion rate is small, climate impacts from coal combustion emissions are building quickly, and annual reductions in those emissions must occur at high rates if ecosystem-threatening consequences are to be avoided. Similarly, in the case of petrochemical pollution, merely to reduce the dispersion of plastics and other petrochemicals into the environment by the annual rate of depletion of oil and natural gas would not avert environmental harms on a scale that could lead to the collapse of ecosystems and human societies.

Where reduction in emissions or other pollutants can be obtained without reducing non-renewable resource consumption, for example, by capturing polluting substances and sequestering them, or by curtailing the production of certain industrial chemicals, then a reduction in consumption of such resources need only occur at the depletion rate to achieve sustainability. However, society should be extremely skeptical and careful regarding claims for untested technologies' abilities to safely sequester polluting substances for very long periods of time.

This axiom builds upon Natural Step condition 2.

Evaluation

These axioms are of course open to further refinement. I have attempted to anticipate likely criticisms, which will probably say these axioms are not sufficient to define the concept of sustainability. The most obvious of these is worth mentioning and discussing here: *Why is there no axiom relating to social equity* (similar to the Natural Step's fourth condition)?

The purpose of the axioms set forth here is not to describe conditions that would lead to a good or just society, but to a society that can be maintained over time. It is not clear that perfect economic equality or a perfectly egalitarian system of decision-making is necessary to avert societal collapse. Certainly, extreme inequality seems to make societies vulnerable to internal social and political upheaval. On the other hand, it could be argued that a society's adherence to these five axioms will tend to lead to relatively greater levels of economic and political equality, thus obviating the need for a separate axiom in this regard. In anthropological literature, modest rates of resource consumption and low population sizes relative to the available resource base are correlated with the use of egalitarian decision-making processes and with economic equity — though the correlation is skewed by other variables, such as means of sustenance (hunting and gathering societies tend to be highly equitable and egalitarian, while pastoral societies tend to be less so). If such correlations continue to hold, the reversion to lower rates of resource consumption should lead to a more rather than less egalitarian society.[14]

Will local, national, and international leaders ever shape public policy according to these five axioms? Clearly, policies that would require an end to population growth—and perhaps even a population decline — as well as a reduction in the consumption of resources would not be welcomed, unless the general populace could be persuaded of the necessity of making its activities sustainable. However, if leaders do not begin to abide by these axioms, society as a whole, or some aspects of it, will assuredly collapse. Perhaps knowledge of this fact is sufficient incentive to overcome the psychological and political resistance that would otherwise frustrate efforts toward true sustainability.

5

Parrots and Peoples

A RECENT DOCUMENTARY FILM by Judy Irving, *The Wild Parrots of Telegraph Hill,* and the book of the same title by Mark Bittner,[1] have few obvious implications for global war or peace, resource depletion, or worldwide economic meltdown. Nevertheless, they've gotten me to musing about avians, freedom, and civilization in ways that may be relevant to those topics.

Bittner, a native of Washington State, moved to San Francisco in the early 1970s with the goal of pursuing a musical career. His dreams were dashed by the ugly realities of the commercial music scene and he ended up homeless. Refusing to seek regular employment, he subsisted for years on handouts and odd jobs, eventually landing a caretaking position in a small house on Telegraph Hill, leaving him plenty of free time.

A devotee of spiritual literature and Beat poets, Bittner imagined himself one day being a professional writer and living in wild nature — somewhere among rivers, mountains, and trees. Yet now he found himself stuck without money in a starkly urban environment, and without any motivation to improve his financial situation by the conventional means.

One day, while reading an interview with Gary Snyder in the collection *The Real Work,* Bittner came upon the following passage:

> The city is just as natural as the country, let's not forget it. There's nothing in the universe that's not natural by

Mark Bittner with a wild conure friend. Credit: Jocelyn Knight

definition. One of the poems I like best in *Turtle Island* is "Night Herons," which is about the naturalness of San Francisco.[2]

Bittner writes: "There was an implication for me that I caught immediately: If I were really sincere about knowing nature, I'd start right where I was living." So he began observing birds.

One day in 1990, by chance he saw four wild parrots; in the following weeks, more appeared. He was intrigued by them. Where had they come from? He had been paying attention to the pigeons, sparrows, and seagulls around the rambling gardens near his cottage, but was unable to summon up much real interest in them. The parrots were different. They were obviously non-native, and were "always good for a laugh."

They would fly into the garden with their nutty urgency, a united, harmonious group. Then, the instant they landed, fights would break out. Sometimes while fighting they'd get tangled up in each other's feet and fall from the lines, struggling to disengage before both birds crashed to the ground. They were affectionate with one another, too. Pairs had long preening sessions, at the end of which they'd puff up their feathers and sit cheek to cheek.

Bittner's book is essentially a diary of his interactions with the birds during the following years; Irving's film, though necessarily containing far less detail, conveys the visual and auditory impact of parrots playing, fighting, flying, and interacting with their adopted human friend.

And friendship is a good term for what develops. Bittner is keenly aware that most North Americans experience parrots only as caged birds, but he gains a deep respect for this flock's freedom. Bittner himself has, after all, eluded the domesticating process entailed in getting a regular job and working for a living. He himself has experienced just enough freedom to understand why the parrots relish their wildness and vigorously repel any attempt to cage or tame them.

Yet both Bittner and the flock exist in a state of paradox: they are wild animals — in Bittner's case, only metaphorically so — within a largely domesticated environment. They are non-natives who are doing their best to make their way in an ecosystem for which they have not evolved. They gratefully accept whatever sustenance they get via the kindness of strangers, but only on their own terms: they insist on maintaining control of their own existence.

The parrots, mostly cherry-headed conures (also known as red-masked parakeets), have come from South America. There, presumably, they had been trapped in the wild. A few may briefly have been kept as pets before escaping (or being deliberately turned loose by their frustrated "owners"); the rest were born and fledged in the wild — not in their native habitat, but in the gardens and parks of San Francisco.

Bittner finds himself committed to a strange vocation. He is an uncredentialed ethologist and amateur ornithologist. And his commitment is considerable: he spends hours each day with the parrots, feeding and observing them. He takes copious notes; he saves up money for film so that he can photograph them; and he occasionally resorts to soliciting donations from the neighborhood when a parrot falls ill and needs a veterinarian's attention. The parrots become his closest comrades.

Throughout the book and film we get to know individual birds and learn their stories. We are witness to their courtships, alliances, disputes, births, illnesses, and deaths. Among others, we get to know Connor, the blue-crowned conure, who, though somewhat of an outcast because he is of a different species than the rest, maintains a dignified, kind presence; Tupelo, a victim of a virus that recurs each year in the younger birds, whom Bittner takes into his home, nurses, and becomes deeply attached to; and Mingus, an escaped cherry-head pet who joins the flock and then takes up residence in Bittner's cottage, eschewing life on the wing. Mingus has the infuriating habit of biting, but displays the endearing trait of bopping his head up and down in perfect time whenever Bittner plays the guitar and sings.

The most striking aspect of this narrative is having a window into parrot society, and into the emotional lives of individual birds. Here's a summary paragraph from Bittner:

> Parrot society is complex, but I don't think it is so different from ours. It's a community made up of pairs and individuals. Mated birds squabble with one another and with other couples. Certain individuals have it in for each other. Most couples are in it for the long term, but some get divorced. Although the flock functions as a single community, nobody makes decisions for the flock as a whole. When a parrot thinks it's time to leave a foraging spot, he starts up a conversation about it. If the flock leaves, it's a community decision. Often, some birds will dissent from the general consensus and stay put.

The book brims with charming anecdotes about bird behavior. Just one: When a lone little budgie ("Smitty") briefly joins the flock, nearly all of the other birds shun it. Connor, however, befriends the parakeet, letting it eat crumbs he drops and even occasionally holding a piece of food with his foot so that the much smaller bird can bite into it. This is behavior that is difficult to explain in strict Darwinian terms. What was Connor getting from the relationship? Surely not enhanced survival chances or reproductive success.

As I savored Bittner's account of the wild parrots, I couldn't help but think back on what I've read over the years about wild humans — that is, about descriptions of hunter-gatherer society, or life among tribal peoples at the time of first European contact.

Take for example, this passage from Baron de Lahontan conveying the statement of a Huron from the end of the 17th century: "We are born free and united brothers, each as much a great lord as the other, while you are all the slaves of one sole man. I am the master of my body, I dispose of myself. I do what I wish. I am the first and the last of my Nation...subject only to the great Spirit."

The analogy is inescapable: people who live a civilized life are like birds in a cage. As long as we stay within well-defined social bounds (and assuming we are lucky enough to have been born in a wealthy parasitic society, rather than a victimized poor one), we are rewarded with cheap food as well as comfort and convenience in a myriad of forms: television, shopping malls, glossy magazines. We have our seed cup, perch, mirror, and toys. What more could a bird — or human — want?

Moreover, life in the wild is unpredictable. There are hawks waiting to snatch us (life as a wild parrot, thrush, or finch is like living in an apartment building with neighbors who happen to be serial-killing cannibals). But, of course, we civilized humans have managed to extinguish just about all of the large predators who might otherwise make off with the occasional child, sick cousin, or doddering grandfather. The only predators we have to worry about now are other people.

Salish men stand by tepees near St. Ignatius Mission, Flathead Reservation, Montana, July 4th 1903. Credit: Northwest Museum of Arts and Culture

Like wild parrot society, wild hunter-gatherer society could be fraught with conflict. Fights evidently arose over sexual jealousy, food, and etiquette.

According to Raymond C. Kelly's calculations in his book *Warless Societies and the Origin of War*, the typical rate of homicides among even the more peaceful foraging societies was in the range of 40 to 90 fatalities per 100,000 persons per year.[3] Compare that with the homicide rates of modern America (5.5 per 100,000), Germany (1.1), or the Netherlands (0.75). In civilized society we have police, laws, courts, and prisons to keep the lid on interpersonal mayhem. However, we also have occasional wars, which can be horrifyingly lethal (one in every fifty individuals died during World War II; the American Civil War had a similar fatality rate). If I were living in Iraq these days, I might find the statistical likelihood of violent death in hunter-gatherer society decidedly preferable to my own odds.

For whatever reasons, most of us modern humans are like Mingus the parrot: we choose domesticated life. We like the cheap food, the controlled environment. Yet while life in the wild isn't

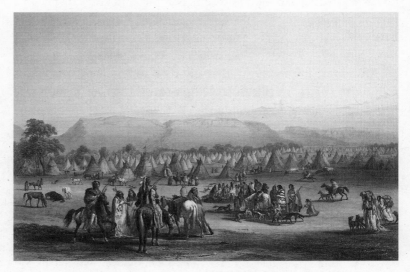

Encampment of the Peikann Indians 1840–1843. Credit: Library of Congress.

easy, it has an ecstatic quality, one that Bittner notes among the parrots, and one that early explorers observed among the Native Americans and Aboriginal Australians. It is a quality that cannot survive the routines of either civilization or the cage.

So how did we arrive at civilization in the first place? It's a long story, but one worth rehearsing periodically so as to remind ourselves why we traded away our freedom.

Every competent hunter-gatherer knows how to survive in the wild; therefore, if anyone in the band starts to lord it over his comrades, they can simply pick up and leave. No one can threaten to withhold food from anyone who is not an infant or an invalid. The situation differs in an agriculture-supported city. As we developed food production (horticulture, then agriculture — presumably because we had gotten so good at hunting, and our populations had grown so dense, that we could no longer easily support ourselves except by planting and harvesting), seasonal surpluses provided an incentive for raids, and thus for political organization to protect from raids (or to organize them). Individuals found themselves in a social pyramid composed of peasants who produced food and paid tribute

Punca or Ponca indians encamped on the banks of the Missouri, 1840.
Credit: Library of Congress.

(a portion of the crop was collected and stored by a managerial elite); a middle class composed of various specialists (soldiers, accountants, traders, artists, artisans, lawyers, scribes, and religious functionaries); and the decision-making leadership made up of kings and queens and their families.

Thus with full-time division of labor came a new form of political organization: the state. On one level, it justified itself by managing seasonal surpluses and redistributing them in times of famine. But at the same time, the state was a protection racket: as sociologist Max Weber argued, it is the element within society that claims a legitimate monopoly on the use of violence.[4] Soldiers, police, prison guards, and executioners represent the business end of state power, without which the rest of the edifice could hardly function.

As cities took up the space formerly occupied by untamed nature, the survival options of wild people diminished. Individuals gradually lost their ability to live outside their artificial, controlled environments. Of course, to this day everyone is still ultimately dependent on nature, but now only indirectly. We look to the social system for our sustenance; we chase money, not rabbits.

Hupa man with spear, standing on rock midstream; in background, fog partially obscures trees on mountainsides. Credit: Edward S. Curtis (Library of Congress)

This disconnection from wild nature was especially acute in those who were not members of the producing class — the soldiers, managers, priests, poets, and kings who didn't work in the fields all day, and who therefore didn't have to pay such close attention to weather, soil, birds, wolves, deer, and gophers.

At first, these specialists and overlords made up a small minority of the population. In an agrarian society, surpluses are small and the work of food production must be done by muscle power, so that lots of human labor is needed. But with the industrial revolution, fossil fuels replaced muscle power, and so ever more people could be "freed" from agricultural work. The middle classes burgeoned, while the number of producers declined.

And so here we are today, in a human world dominated by money, news, sports, entertainment, employment, and investment — a world in which nature appears as something peripheral and mostly unnecessary. Nature is merely a pile of resources, a segment of the economy, at best something to be preserved for aesthetic or sentimental reasons.

But in domesticating plants and animals we also domesticated ourselves. Certain personalities were selected for, others discouraged. The abilities to conform and to delay gratification were selected for (at least among the producing and middle classes); the insistence on autonomy and freedom was discouraged. Meanwhile we domesticated other animals with similar objectives in mind: we wanted docile pets or willing field workers.

Again: we are like caged birds — except that our captors are others like ourselves. In effect, we have built our own cages.

When Bittner occasionally comes across a parrot that he knows was hand-raised, he notices the difference between it and its wild cousins. At one point he is offered the "ownership" of a captive blue-crowned conure named Bucky. He immediately accepts the bird, hoping to have found a mate for Connor — a solitary blue-crown who has led a lonely existence in the red-crowned flock. Bucky turns out to be another male, but never mind: both birds are at first delighted to be in each other's company. Yet gradually their relationship sours: Bucky is unsuited to life in the wild, while Connor is loath to give up his freedom. Bittner comments on Bucky's "chronic possessiveness":

> On rare occasions, [Connor] would spend the night out with the flock, but he always returned the next morning. Bucky didn't want Connor going out at all. Whenever I reached into their cage to get Connor, Bucky would bite

my hand and then pin Connor up against the cage wall and bite him and preen him. His meaning was intuitively clear: "Don't go, I love you." It was a neurotic, clinging kind of love that I think only a caged bird could have.

On the subject of freedom versus captivity Bittner writes:

> While I don't believe hand-reared birds should be released — they would not survive — I have a big problem with people who think they have a right to put a healthy wild bird in a cage. Birds cherish their freedom just as much as human beings do. The sick parrots that I brought inside always screamed in terror and despair at the moment of capture. Each time a parrot is taken out of the wild, a family — the members of which feel real affection for one another — gets broken up.

If only European pioneers had harbored similar sentiments about the wild peoples they encountered.

As Bittner points out in his book, ornithologists are unsure about the descent of parrots, which have no clear relatives among other birds and must have diverged from some unknown common avian progenitor many millions of years ago. There are about 330 recognized parrot species in the world (most are endangered) — birds large and small, displaying nearly every color of the rainbow. All share the defining characteristics of hooked bill, the presence of a *cere* (a band of flesh above the upper mandible), and zygodactylic feet (two toes point forward, two backward).

As all parrot lovers know, these birds are eerily intelligent and endlessly entertaining. They are natural clowns, spending much of their time in play and other social behavior.

Captive parrots can, of course, be trained to talk. But there is some controversy as to whether their speech is necessarily limited to mere mimicry, or whether it can develop into genuine communication of concepts and abstractions. For many years Dr. Irene Pepperberg of the University of Arizona has worked with an African grey parrot named Alex who has learned to describe unfamiliar objects, ask for what he wants, and verbalize his own emotional states in English.[5] Alex has become famous for his abilities, but critics have suggested that he is merely a fluke. So Pepperberg and her graduate students are using their methods to train other parrots to do the same things. They are also using rigorous controls to avoid cueing the birds via the "clever Hans" effect. Alex and his avian colleagues evince numeric cognition, categorization and word comprehension among other abilities previously assumed to exist perhaps among the great apes, but certainly not among birds.

"What matter is orange and three-cornered?" Pepperberg asks Alex.

Alex is permitted to examine several objects on a tray before answering. They consist of differently shaped pieces of cloth and other materials in varying colors.

"Want a nut," he says.

"I know, I'll give you a nut," replies Pepperberg.

"Wanna go back," says Alex, meaning into his cage.

Pepperberg loses patience. "C'mon Alex," she implores.

Alex replies, "I'm sorry."[6]

In San Francisco the cherry-headed conure is a non-native species. What would happen if it proliferated there? That's a fair question. After all, look at what has befallen North American songbirds because of the starling, another bird that was introduced by humans — in this case, from Europe (Mozart was reputed to have had a pet starling of which he was particularly fond). Starlings crowd out the natives in cities and suburbs across the continent. One could imagine a local ecological horror story in the case of parrots as well. Suppose the San Francisco wild conures were to thrive, finding niches throughout the West Coast. Might they displace towhees, goldfinches, or hummingbirds?

That's not likely to happen: few introduced species are as successful as the starling. And if the conures of Telegraph Hill do manage to survive, they will have achieved a certain poetic justice. After all, it's not as if parrots are entirely strangers to North America. The continent once had its own native parrot, the Carolina parakeet, which was driven to extinction in 1918 by farmers and sportsmen who shot the birds by the tens of thousands. From a parrot's point of view, the conures' colonization of San Francisco's urban ecosystem might be seen as making up for lost territory.

Of course, the most threatening non-native species of all is Homo sapiens. The vast majority of successful colonizing species have arrived in their new habitats because of deliberate or inadvertent human action. And humans themselves — by killing "pests" and "weeds" and encouraging the growth of the few plants and animals they (we) have domesticated — take up the ecological space of thousands of creatures.

Invasive species typically don't follow the local ecological rules by which native species have evolved. Relatively undisturbed ecosystems tend to reach a climax phase, characterized by balanced predator/prey feedback loops that keep population fluctuations within a moderate range and give rise to what appears to be widespread cooperation among species. Invasive plants or animals upset these balances and often compete ruthlessly with natives. Invaded ecosystems have to adjust to the intruders, and this can take years, decades, or centuries.

We humans have upset habitats everywhere we have gone, starting in the Pleistocene. Twenty or thirty thousand years ago we managed to get pretty good at making and using weapons like spears and spear throwers, which enabled us to kill big animals such as mammoths and mastodons. As we spread around the world we killed off one species of megafauna after another. Only after staying in particular places for millennia did we learn the local limits and develop cultural forms that enjoined us to conserve. Evidence suggests that the Native Americans and Aboriginal Australians didn't start out as intuitive ecologists; they learned that attitude as the result of trial and error.

I've been spending a lot of time in airports and airplanes lately as I travel far and wide to spread information about Peak Oil, so I tend to spend less time at home. I do get to meet interesting people, but the wear and tear is undeniable. Indeed, much of this essay was written on planes and buses, in airports and hotels.

These are about as "unnatural" as any environment one can find. Here it is difficult to take Gary Snyder's words, quoted above (p. 97), seriously: there is little or no evidence of wildness in the conventional sense to be found in any of these places (when I was in the Tucson airport recently I noted some wayward sparrows chirping anxiously in the rafters of the ticketing lobby; while it was a pleasure to hear and see them in that sterile environment, I feared for these lost creatures). Of course, in the broadest sense, as Snyder argues, everything people do is "natural," including building and inhabiting airports, since people are no less biological organisms than are bacteria, scorpions, possums, sparrows, or parrots.

At the same time, the distinction between "natural" and "unnatural" does make sense at some level. At the core of the category of the "unnatural" is the human social construct described above (p. 103) — that of full-time division of labor in a context of agricultural production and city-building.

Why have no other animals built equivalent civilizations? Why no parrot skyscrapers, symphonies, or supermarkets? For better or worse, we humans have certain unique genetically endowed abilities. We are omnivorous — so, like other omnivores (crows, raccoons, rats, cockroaches) we are clever and adaptable. We have a descended larynx that enables us to make a wide variety of vocal sounds — hence language. And we have opposable thumbs that enable us easily to make and use tools. With language and cleverness we get the abilities to generalize and to plan ahead. Combine those abilities with ever-evolving tool systems and the results are formidable.

While parrots can be trained to speak in context, most linguists would say that this is still qualitatively different from human verbal communication. And of course it is. But contemplating what that difference is and how it might have arisen brings up the questions: Did humans develop language and tools *because* they are special and different from other animals? Or did humans *become* special in their own eyes because they developed language and tools? Most people assume the former, but doing so just seems to widen the gulf between ourselves and the rest of nature.

It is easy to dislike human beings in the aggregate. Hearing about the endemic torture at Abu Ghraib prison in Iraq and the global destruction of species (about a quarter of mammals and birds are now threatened), or any of a thousand other outrages, one can catch oneself hoping that Earth will simply be rid of our kind soon.

But Bittner reminds us there is more to humans than this. He tries to remain an objective, detached observer of parrots in order to gain credibility, but eventually he has to admit to himself (and his readers) that the reason he spends time with the birds is that he loves them — and not merely in some abstract spiritual or aesthetic sense. It is love that keeps him interested in the daily lives of specific birds with which he forms life-long bonds. It is love that keeps the flock together, love that enables it to grow. Human society is similar: without affection, we couldn't overcome our competitiveness long enough to accomplish much of anything. Moreover, it is our ability to extend this bond of empathy, compassion, interest, and fellow-feeling across species barriers that may offer us one of our last opportunities for escape from our self-designed cage, and one of our last chances to veer away from our ecocidal path. This sounds pretty sappy, I know. We've all heard it a million times: it's love that gives us meaning and that makes life worthwhile. And people are capable of extraordinary displays of love in a myriad of forms. Maybe it takes a flock of parrots to drive the point home.

At the end of the book and film we are treated to a pleasant surprise: Mark finds a girlfriend. He has also become a successful author and the subject of a documentary film. He has achieved success — though by a long, circuitous, and initially unpromising route. He has stuck to his vision and his principles. He has (mostly) avoided the cage.

Both the book and the film tell us as much about ourselves as they do about parrots. We are a peculiar species of ape, evidently not closely related to birds (genetically, we're closer to voles than to parrots). Yet in the conures of Telegraph Hill we see reflections of ourselves — as we are, as we were, and as we may once again be. And we are reminded just how lonely it can be to confine our attention solely to the solipsistic human matrix, when so much more is going on around us.

6

Population, Resources, and Human Idealism

U RINETOWN is a funny, smart, Tony award-winning musical. Its action takes place in a city of the future where, as the result of severe and ongoing water shortages, private toilets have been banned. A giant corporation, the Urine Good Company (UGC for short), is in charge of all pay-per-pee services. The gradually escalating price is still affordable to a well-off few, but teeming masses of the poor have to scrape together piles of spare change every day in order to take care of their private business. This, announces policeman-narrator Officer Lockstock, is "the central conceit of the show."

The cast includes a greedy villain (Caldwell B. Cladwell, the CEO of UGC), a courageous hero (Bobby Strong, a poor lad who works for UGC collecting fees at a down-scale public toilet), and a big-hearted heroine (Hope, Cladwell's daughter). Bobby and Hope fall in love; Bobby leads a rebellion against UGC; "terrorists" take Hope hostage. She sings the uplifting "Follow Your Heart," assuring herself and everyone else that love will win the day, but every line is tongue-in-cheek. Though Bobby is soon killed by UGC minions, Hope manages to gain ultimate power, disposing of her father and telling her followers that the time of deprivation is over. In the last scene she sings the fervent anthem "I See a River," envisioning a new era when all can pee as much as they like, whenever they like, wherever they like. However, by the end of the scene the entire cast — excepting the narrator — has perished in an ecological catastrophe brought on by overpopulation. Officer Lockstock's epilogue tells the sorry tale:

> Of course, it wasn't long before the water became silty, brackish, and then dried up altogether. Cruel as Caldwell B. Cladwell was, his measures effectively regulated water consumption.... Hope, however, chose to ignore the warning signs, choosing instead to bask in the people's love as long as it lasted. Hope eventually joined her father in a manner not quite so gentle. As for the people of this town? Well, they did the best they could. But they were prepared for the world they inherited.... For when the water dried up, they recognized their town for the first time for what it really was. What it was always waiting to be...

The Chorus sings: "This is Urinetown! Always it's been Urinetown! This place it's called Urinetown!" And with their unison cry of "Hail Malthus!", the curtain falls.

The entire play is a send-up of the musical comedy genre, and the audience goes home laughing at gags and humming memorable

tunes. Many reviewers have emphasized the infectious zaniness of the play, seemingly missing its explicit message — idealism and good intentions are insufficient responses to problems of population pressure and resource depletion. Maybe that's just as well: *Urinetown* succeeds so well as comedy and theater that even people utterly immune to its insights still have a good time; thus more people are drawn to see it, including those who *do* "get it."

Thomas Malthus 1766–1834. Credit: Public Domain

What's the significance of the play's last line, "Hail Malthus!"?

Thomas Malthus (1766–1834) was a British political economist who theorized that unchecked population growth must eventually outstrip increases in food production. He is most famous for the *Essay on Population* (1798), in which he explained in simple terms the connection between population pressure and human misery. The following passage from "The History of Economic Thought" website summarizes his ideas succinctly:

> Actual (checked) population growth is kept in line with food supply growth by "positive checks" (starvation, disease and the like, elevating the death rate) and "preventive checks" (i.e. postponement of marriage, etc. that keep down the birthrate), both of which are characterized by "misery and vice." Malthus's hypothesis implied that actual population always has a *tendency* to push above the food supply. Because of this tendency, any attempt to ameliorate the condition of the lower classes by increasing their incomes or improving agricultural productivity would be fruitless, as the extra means of subsistence would be completely absorbed by an induced boost in population. As long as this tendency remains, Malthus argued, the "perfectibility" of society will always be out of reach.[1]

No wonder the term *Malthusian* almost always has negative connotations. Indeed, Malthus became anathema to utopians of the left and right, who envision a world with no limits. He has been reviled as a "hard-hearted monster," a "prophet of doom," and an "enemy of the working class."

The summary goes on:

> In his much-expanded and revised 1803 edition of the *Essay,* Malthus concentrated on bringing empirical evidence to bear (much of it acquired on his extensive travels to Germany, Russia and Scandinavia). He also introduced the possibility of "moral restraint" (voluntary abstinence which leads to neither misery nor vice) bringing the unchecked population growth rate down to a point where

the tendency is gone. In practical policy terms, this meant inculcating the lower classes with middle-class virtues. He believed this could be done with the introduction of universal suffrage, state-run education for the poor and, more controversially, the elimination of the Poor Laws and the establishment of an unfettered nation-wide labor market. He also argued that once the poor had a taste for luxury, then they would demand a higher standard of living for themselves before starting a family. Thus . . . Malthus is suggesting the possibility of "demographic transition," i.e. that sufficiently high incomes may be enough by themselves to reduce fertility.

Malthus believed that a general famine would occur in the near future unless his policies were implemented; in this he was clearly wrong. There have indeed been localized famines in the decades since his death (e.g., in Ireland, the Soviet Union, China, North Korea, and Ethiopia), but these have provided only a minor brake on global population, which has surged by over 500 percent in the interim. This failure of prediction is the main cudgel wielded by generations of Malthus-bashers, who attribute the growth of world food production over the past century-and-a-half primarily to human ingenuity. As knowledge expands, so does our ability to sustain more people.

But increased knowledge and cleverness can account for only a portion of the added global human carrying capacity. The main factor has been the use of fossil fuels for clearing land, pumping irrigation water, fueling tractors and other farm equipment, fertilizing soils, killing pests, and transporting produce ever further distances to support people in remote urban centers who would be otherwise unable to sustain themselves. Malthus could hardly have foreseen the contributions of fossil fuels to economic expansion and population growth during the past two centuries. And so, taking into account the inevitable, now-commencing winding down of that brief, incomparably opulent fossil-fuel fiesta, it may be better to say that Malthus wasn't wrong, he was just ahead of his time.

But if the depletion of fossil fuels proves Malthus to have been ultimately correct in his forecast of human die-off, what would that say for the rest of his message — his calls to abolish the Poor Laws and thus, in Bill Clinton's famous locution, "end welfare as we know it," and his implicit view that the "perfectibility of society will always be out of reach"?

William Stanton is a retired geologist and contemporary author who has taken up Malthus's mantle in a well-researched but grim and controversial book, *The Rapid Growth of Human Populations, 1750–2000*. In it, he compiles population data on virtually every nation: each page features a country chart accompanied by a paragraph or two describing the unique historical circumstances that caused the line on the graph to assume its particular shape. Want to know the population history of the Maldives? The chart and explanatory paragraphs are on page 196. These typically take up about half of each page; the other half is devoted to the running text, a sometimes highly opinionated discussion of population and resources.

A thorough and proud Malthusian, Stanton also takes an uncompromising stance against multiculturalism, the welfare state, and immigration: he considers conventional liberal attitudes toward these as forms of "sentimentality" that only make humanity's problems worse. Here are some representative passages:

> Compassion is a luxury available to people enjoying peace and plenty, who are confident of their place in society.... They apply it to the hungry, needy, or oppressed. It makes them feel virtuous — until the needy try to take advantage of the givers.... Human 'rights' often conflict with each other. For example, if a couple insists on their 'right' to have lots of babies, the family that results may lose its 'right' to enjoy a comfortable standard of living....[2]

In a more recent essay, "Oil and People," published in the Association for the Study of Peak Oil and Gas (ASPO) newsletter #55 (July 2005), Stanton writes:

So the population reduction scenario with the best chance of success has to be Darwinian in all its aspects, with none of the sentimentality that shrouded the second half of the 20th Century in a dense fog of political correctness.... The Darwinian approach, in this planned population reduction scenario, is to maximize the well-being of the UK as a nation-state. Individual citizens, and aliens, must expect to be seriously inconvenienced by the single-minded drive to reduce population ahead of resource shortage. The consolation is that the alternative, letting Nature take its course, would be so much worse.

The scenario is: Immigration is banned. Unauthorized arrivals are treated as criminals. Every woman is entitled to raise one healthy child. No religious or cultural exceptions can be made, but entitlements can be traded. Abortion or infanticide is compulsory if the fetus or baby proves to be handicapped (Darwinian selection weeds out the unfit). When, through old age, accident or disease, an individual becomes more of a burden than a benefit to society, his or her life is humanely ended. Voluntary euthanasia is legal and made easy. Imprisonment is rare, replaced by corporal punishment for lesser offences and painless capital punishment for greater.[3]

In subsequent online discussions, Stanton was excoriated for these statements. One writer, identified only by pseudonym, accused Stanton of far-right political leanings, using terms I am unable to reprint as they may be considered libelous in some countries.

Colin Campbell, ASPO's founder, had the last word in the discussion:

I think [Stanton] was proposing some sort of managed decline (as for example by hanging criminals) rather than just letting Nature take its course in which the strong eat the weak. I think he was simply suggesting how Britain might react and achieve in isolation the reduction imposed by Nature. I don't think there was anything particularly xenophobic: the Nigerians would be equally free to solve their same problem however they might. . . .

Al Bartlett, retired professor of physics at the University of Colorado, developed a lecture in the early 1970s that he has since delivered over 1,600 times. Titled *Arithmetic, Population, and Energy,* the talk explores the meaning of steady growth (so many percent per year), which is of course the sacred basis of all modern economies.[4] As Bartlett makes clear, *no* steady rate of growth in population or resource consumption is sustainable.

During the course of the lecture, he asks, "Well, what can we do about this? What makes the population problem worse, and what reduces it?" On the screen he projects a slide with two columns of words. In the left-hand column are the principal factors leading to population growth; in the right, factors leading to a decrease of population.

Bartlett notes that population growth will cease at some point: the mathematics assures us of that. Moreover, we need not do anything to solve the population problem; nature will take care of that for us. Sooner or later, from the right-hand column nature will choose some method or methods of limiting human numbers. But the options chosen may not be to our liking. The only way we can

Table of Options

Increase Populations	Decrease Populations
Procreation	Abstention
Motherhood	Contraception/Abortion
Large Families	Small families
Immigration	Stopping Immigration
Medicine	
Public Health	Disease
Sanitation	
Peace	War
Law and Order	Murder/Violence
Scientific Agriculture	Famine
Accident Prevention	Accidents
Clean Air	Pollution (Smoking)
Ignorance of the Problem	

avoid having to live with (or die by) nature's choices is to proactively choose for ourselves which options from the right-hand column we would prefer voluntarily to implement. Hesitating in our choice, or failing to implement it, merely forces nature's hand.

Toward the end of his lecture, Bartlett quotes Isaac Asimov, from an interview with Bill Moyers recorded in 1989. Moyers asked Asimov, "What happens to the idea of the dignity of the human species if this population growth continues at its present rate?" Asimov replied:

> It will be completely destroyed. I like to use what I call my bathroom metaphor: if two people live in an apartment and there are two bathrooms, then both have freedom of the bathroom. You can go to the bathroom anytime you want to stay as long as you want for whatever you need. And everyone believes in freedom of the bathroom; it should be right there in the Constitution. But if you have twenty people in the apartment and two bathrooms, no matter how much every person believes in freedom of the bathroom, there is no such thing. You have to set up times for each person, you have to bang on the door, Aren't you through yet? and so on. In the same way, democracy cannot survive overpopulation. Human dignity cannot survive [overpopulation]. Convenience and decency cannot survive [overpopulation]. As you put more and more people onto the world, the value of life not only declines, it disappears. It doesn't matter if someone dies, the more people there are, the less one person matters.

Urinetown, indeed.

All of this is dreary and distressing, and that's why most people prefer simply to avoid the topic. None of us *wants* to have to choose anything from Bartlett's second column. Even the most agreeable items (abstention, abortion, contraception, and small families) are controversial, especially if proposed as anything other than individual, voluntary options. Controlling immigration, which is essential to enabling any nation to control domestic population growth, is enormously controversial, as immigrants already often face discrimination in many forms. In each case, one or another group would object that human rights are being sacrificed. Yet nature does not negotiate: the Earth is a bounded sphere, and human population growth and consumption growth *will be* reined in. So it appears we must give up at least *some* human rights if we are to avoid nature's solutions — which have traditionally consisted of famine and disease, as well as the instinctive human response to fight over scarce resources.

Should we then throw human rights to the wind, as Stanton seems to do? Capital punishment, compulsory infanticide, or abortion — wouldn't adopting these as policy be equivalent to rolling back two or more centuries of gains in humanitarian thinking and social practice? And could such policies ever gain hold in a truly democratic society, or does the avoidance of demographic collapse thus also imply authoritarian governance?

I don't think it has to. And I'm not about to give up on humanitarianism. But there is an essential lesson here. If we want peace, democracy, and human rights, we must work to create the ecological condition essential for these things to exist: i.e., a stable human population at — or *less than* — the environment's long-term carrying capacity.

This is a lesson that earlier humans internalized, to one degree or another. But during the first half of the fossil-fuel era we could afford to forget it: we were creating new temporary carrying capacity left and right. We could dream of "freedom of the bathroom" — human rights to food, education, health care, housing, and so on — no matter how many of us there were. Now, as that phantom carrying capacity is set to disappear, and as the human population is overshooting the natural limits of topsoil, water, fish, and fuels, the ideals we have come to hold are being threatened.

I do not advocate an absolute ecological determinism (as Stanton seems very close to doing): faced with population pressure and resource depletion, some societies do better than others (at least temporarily) at maintaining a humane social environment. Peak Oil won't necessarily lead to *Soylent Green* — unless we ignore the lesson.

To do so — to think that we can advocate for human rights, peace, and social justice while ignoring their necessary ecological basis — is both intellectually dishonest and ultimately self-defeating.

The longer we put off choosing the nicer methods of achieving demographic stability, the more likely the nasty ones become, whether imposed by nature or by some fascistic regime. Urine Good Company might represent a mild version of what could actually be in store if we let the marketplace, corporations, and secretive, militaristic governments come up with eugenic solutions to our population dilemma.

The proponents of fascistic "solutions" (I'm not suggesting that Stanton is in that category, by the way) are likely to justify their calls for war and ethnic cleansing with an appeal to human nature: we must abandon our recently acquired squeamishness and sentimentality and do what any self-respecting caveman would have done when faced with a resource crisis — make sure that it is *they* who starve or are exterminated, and that it is *our* children who survive, and thus *our* genes that are passed along.

Human nature does indeed contain the potential for demographic competition, even to the point of genocide. But it is important to remember that the real "cavemen" — our hunter-gatherer ancestors — lived by sharing and enjoyed a gift economy. Our modern "sentimentality," in the form of concerns for equity and the welfare of those who would otherwise be left behind, is rooted in ancient sensibilities.

Yet while hunter-gatherers embodied the egalitarian ideal, we must remember that their ethic also included the imperative to hew to ecological limits. Infanticide was the last resort when contraception and the suppression of fertility through extended lactation and maintenance of low levels of body fat failed.

An ethic of human rights, of sharing, and of equity *without a practically expressed awareness of ecological limits* is a setup for disaster. But demographic competition by way of fascism, as a response to population-resource crises, is an admission of failure; and it is less an expression of human nature than of the ugly habits formed through the past few thousand civilized years of extreme inequality, hierarchy, and authoritarianism.

The longer we wait, the fewer our options. Social liberals and progressives who fail to talk about population and resource issues and to propose workable solutions are merely helping to create their own worst nightmare.

The End of One Era, the Beginning of Another

7

The Psychology of Peak Oil
and Climate Change

THE HISTORIC, GLOBAL SHIFT from a regime of cheap fossil fuel energy sources to one of declining and expensive fossil fuels and scarce replacements will impact every living person, every community, and every nation. Global Climate Change will similarly affect every human being — and every ecosystem as well. Much of the human impact will be measurable in economic terms; however, individual and collective psychological effects will perhaps be of equal and often greater significance. Generations that have been trained to want or expect easy, quick, automated abundance will find themselves having to adapt instead to a regime in which everything takes longer and requires more effort; in which there will often not be enough fuel or food to go around. How will people respond? How can community leaders prepare to deal with adverse or even desperate psychological reactions?

Other questions raised by the energy transition that have psychological dimensions include: Why do some people seem immediately to understand the importance of over-arching systemic problems like oil depletion and Climate Change, while others react with indifference or denial? And, perhaps most importantly, could the scientific understanding of human psychology help change our collective thinking proactively so as to minimize the chaos and suffering and maximize positive adaptive behavior?

I will not attempt a systematic or exhaustive treatment of these questions; the topic is potentially vast. This essay is intended merely as a summary of what others have already written along these lines, an exploration of related materials that could be relevant, and a venue for floating a few speculative ideas.

Explaining Our Incomprehension

Why are Peak Oil and Climate Change so hard for many people to understand? There are probably many reasons. One often cited (and discussed brilliantly and at length by Robert Ornstein and Paul Ehrlich in their 1989 book *New World New Mind*) is that humans are hard-wired via the reptilian brain for fight-or-flight responses to adversity or danger, but have an innate inability to respond effectively to slowly developing problems that are hard to personalize. Ornstein and Ehrlich suggest that our species, if it is to survive, must quickly improve its capacity to understand and deal with systemic crises.

Another possible reason why so many people can't "get" Peak Oil and Climate Change has to do with psychological maturity — which often does not correlate particularly well with chronological age. Psychological maturity might be defined as the ability or tendency to think of not just one's own welfare but that of larger groups — family, community, the world as a whole, and that of other species; and to think in terms of long time horizons in addition to short ones. This includes thinking about consequences of present behavior that will be felt only by future generations. People who are psychologically mature know — not just theoretically, but by experience — that youth and old age are on a continuum; that life consists also of death; and that personal sacrifice is sometimes required for the sake of family or community.

Acceptance and Beyond: Peak Oil Grief

The late Swiss-born psychiatrist Elisabeth Kübler-Ross, author of the pathbreaking book *On Death and Dying*, is famous for distinguishing five psychological stages of grief typically traversed by people who have recently been informed that they have a fatal illness —

denial, anger, bargaining, depression, and acceptance. Knowledge of these stages has enabled counselors more effectively to help individuals deal psychologically with their impending demise. Several Peak Oil authors have suggested that Kübler-Ross's five-stage model could also help in describing and treating our collective distress over the impending loss of our comfortable, energy-guzzling way of life. (Could this be a form of *pre*-traumatic stress disorder?) Many people, upon first "getting" Peak Oil or Climate Change respond by exhibiting one or another of these predictable stages, and denial is most often the first.

If the model holds up, we might find that differing messages are effective for helping people reach the point of accepting our situation, depending on their current stage of adjustment. For example, we should expect people who have just heard about the problems for the first time to try out all of the time-worn denial ploys: "Oh, but technology will come to the rescue. Surely *they* will think of something. What if there's lots more oil out there that just hasn't been discovered? Maybe measured warming patterns are just due to natural climate variability. Perhaps a few degrees of warming will actually be good for us!" If people respond with anger, this may simply be symptomatic of an inner psychological process of adjustment that may require days, weeks, or months to work itself out. We may wish to gently persist in offering information, but in ways appropriate to the stage of adjustment being exhibited.

Even those who have reached the acceptance stage of the process seem to cycle back through previous reactions (I still find myself experiencing denial, anger, bargaining, and depression after years of studying the problem of oil depletion).

For over 30 years eco-philosopher and Buddhist scholar Joanna Macy has led "despair and empowerment" workshops (they are now also called "the work that reconnects") with thousands of veteran environmental and peace activists, as well as Israelis and Palestinians and other groups suffering from long-standing enmity. Her workshops are designed to help participants process more thoroughly, quickly, and effectively the grief they feel over the destruction of people and planet, and to overcome the psychology of denial and helplessness that keeps them mired in the status quo. Workshop tools include ritualistic exercises and guided creative processes. In the past few years Joanna has been supportive of Peak Oil education and I've been delighted to offer public presentations with her on a couple of occasions. Some Peak Oil groups in North America and Australia have offered workshops based on her work, including one called "The Heart of Peak Oil" held in Melbourne in 2006.

More than once I've heard the comment that at least some Peak Oil and Climate Change activists seem strangely happy despite the dire nature of their message. Perhaps the Kübler-Ross formula, though useful, is insufficient for the purpose of describing the full cycle of psychological reactions among environmental activists. Beyond acceptance must come a further stage — *action*. Those who simply spend their time learning about oil depletion and the melting of glaciers are often glum plums, the death of a party. However, those who spend hours a week organizing local food systems, car co-ops, and economic localization forums seem to flip over into an infectious cheeriness. This observation, if widely confirmed, could have wider significance: we may have hit upon one of the main potential motivators for broad social change. Knowing the world is unraveling while assuming there's nothing you can do about it is a recipe for desolation. Being involved in heroic work to save the world is empowering and exciting. Once one acknowledges the dilemma we're in, these seem to be the only two options.

Collective PTSD

The next few decades will be traumatic. The slow squeeze of economic contraction will probably be punctuated by dramatic weather-related catastrophes, resource wars, and regional instances of social collapse. As a result, we are likely to see widespread symptoms of post-traumatic stress disorder (PTSD) — a condition first widely recognized among combat soldiers returning from the Vietnam War but now regarded as a generic category of psychological responses to disturbing events ranging from incest to natural disasters. In individuals, the typical symptoms include:

- vigilance and scanning
- elevated startle response
- blunted affect or psychic numbing (the loss of the ability to feel)
- denial (mental reorganization of the event to reduce pain, leading sometimes even to amnesia)
- aggressive, controlling behavior
- interruption of memory and concentration
- depression
- generalized anxiety
- episodes of rage
- substance abuse
- intrusive recall and dissociative "flashback" experiences
- insomnia
- suicidal ideation and
- survivor guilt

In recent years several sociologists and psychologists have investigated collective PTSD — the consequence of an entire society suffering trauma. One of the most extensive surveys of the psychological effects of mass trauma yet published is Lewis Aptekar's *Environmental Disasters in Global Perspective*. Aptekar compared studies from traditional, "developing," and "developed" cultures; he also explored the aftermaths of many kinds of disasters — including chronic disasters (droughts, famines), quick onset disasters (floods, fires, storms, earthquakes), and human-induced disasters (wars, toxic chemical spills, nuclear plant meltdowns). The findings he reviewed are complex and varied, and researchers whose work he cited came to differing conclusions. There is some controversy, for example, on whether the psychological effects of disasters persist for years, perhaps generations, or are only transitory. After a thorough study of researchers' conflicting views, Aptekar concluded that discrepancies in observations probably arise from differences in the nature and severity of the disasters, the presence (or lack) of a social support system, the degree to which the environment returns to its pre-disaster state, as well as from differences in research methods (different studies of the same disaster sometimes produced different results).

Aptekar first dispelled misconceptions about people's immediate responses to disasters. Looting and panic are rare; instead,
people more frequently display behavior that has a clear sense of
purpose and is directed toward the common good. Tragically, officials who believe that social chaos inevitably follows disasters often
delay warning communities of impending crises because they wish
to avoid a panic. Nor do people flee from disaster sites; rather, they
tend to remain. In addition, outsiders usually enter the area in order
to help survivors or to search for family members, producing what
has come to be known as the "convergence phenomenon."

Aptekar described post-traumatic stress disorder in some detail
and cited the work of researchers who studied its impacts in different kinds of natural and human-induced disasters. Symptoms seem
to appear only after the severest disasters, and in cases where victims
are directly and personally affected: "The victims who show the
greatest psychopathology are those who lose close friends and relatives."[1] Not all of the symptoms occur immediately, and reactions
may appear years afterward, especially on anniversaries of the disaster. Gradually, people tend to distort their memory of the event,
forgetting parts of what happened and minimizing its impact and
their reactions to it. Children appear to be particularly vulnerable
after a disaster. Meanwhile, adverse reactions in adults can be so
severe that disaster victims "pass fear and insecurity onto their children—even those yet to be born—by replacing in their child-
rearing a sense of a secure world with a fearful worldview."

One of the early pioneers in the study of disasters, Samuel Prince
(whose work was published in the early 1920s), was convinced that
disasters inevitably bring social change.[2] Subsequent work has
tended to confirm Prince's conclusions; however, the examples
cited by Prince and Aptekar are of non-industrial societies that re-
sponded to trauma by exhibiting more of the characteristics of industrial cultures. This is not likely to be so frequent a response if the
mass trauma consists of a partial or complete collapse of industrialism. Sociologist Max Weber wrote that disasters tend to produce
charismatic leaders, an observation that has been confirmed in vari-

ous cultural settings.[3] This is a social phenomenon that could indeed be extrapolated to the circumstances we can anticipate.

Patterns of reaction in already industrialized societies are somewhat different from those in non-industrial ones. In many instances, impacts are minimized because of the almost immediate availability of elaborate aid and support systems. Yet disaster researcher Benjamin McLuckie hypothesized (in 1977) that "the higher the society's level of technological development, the more vulnerable it would be."[4] That is because people in industrialized countries live in major population centers and rely on sophisticated technologies, increasing their vulnerability to a large-scale collapse of interlocking systems of transportation, communication, water supply, and food distribution.

Responses to human-made disasters are again different: According to Aptekar, victims of these often show *more* stress than victims of natural disasters because of the perceived need to find parties to blame. Whatever the eventual circumstances resulting from Peak Oil and Climate Change, it seems probable that groups in differing geographical areas, and in differing economic conditions, will react in dissimilar ways. In the case of a breakdown of communication and control, those who are more dependent on high tech will likely suffer much more than those who are still somewhat accustomed to locally filling their own basic needs. Over the short term, we are likely to see acts of extraordinary heroism alongside extreme examples of opportunism and stupidity.

But what if the trauma continues for years or decades? To what degree is a persistent, universal disaster (such as the collapse of a society) different from the examples Aptekar cited? In the former case, given enough time, might there indeed be panic and looting, and general flight from the sites of greatest hardship? Aptekar does not offer discussion or examples in this regard; for these we might better look to clues from books like Peter Heather's *The Fall of the Roman Empire*, which discusses, for example, how population levels, especially in Rome itself, fell dramatically, job specialization declined, and famines became more common and severe.

In her essay "Ecological Collapse, Trauma Theory, and Perma-culture," Peak Oil activist Lisa Rayner surveys other relevant lit-erature and draws conclusions directly relevant to the present discussion, quoting frequently from Judith Herman's *Trauma and Recovery*. Other relevant books include Chellis Glendinning's *My Name Is Chellis and I'm in Recovery from Western Civilization* and Benjamin Colodzin's *How to Survive Trauma: A Program for War Veterans and Survivors of Rape, Assault, Abuse or Environmental Disasters*.

Rayner notes that "classic" PTSD refers to responses to an acute life-threatening experience, such as a rape or a severe car accident. However, many people with symptoms of the disorder have not experienced an immediately life-threatening event, but instead have undergone an accumulation of milder stressors. Herman calls this condition "Complex Post Traumatic Stress Disorder," while other researchers refer to it as "Prolonged Duress Stress Disorder (PDSD)."

Rayner points out, "When whole communities suffer from trauma, people develop a kind of mass-PTSD at the social level that makes it very difficult to heal. Alcoholism, domestic violence and other problems become rampant. Conflicts between groups be-come intractable." She also notes that "psychological research shows that it is nearly impossible to heal from past trauma if one is presently in a traumatic situation. For example, a battered wife cannot heal from the effects of child abuse until she gathers the strength to leave her marriage."

In cases where the original trauma is long past, the most impor-tant aspect of treatment seems to be the recollection and emotional processing of the event. A therapist or therapeutic community is often helpful in this regard. Rayner says, "Trauma survivors learn to make some sort of meaning out of their experiences, to take useful lessons about life away from what is otherwise a hopeless and de-grading situation." She quotes Herman's important observation that "recovery can take place only within the context of relation-ships."[5]

All of this suggests that those with psychological training may play as important a role in our collective adaptation to Peak Oil and Climate Change as energy experts and permaculturists. The former should perhaps be gearing up to treat not only individuals but whole communities.

A Model for Explanation and Treatment: Addiction and Dependency

In his January 2006 State of the Union address, George Bush famously observed that "America is addicted to oil." This was news to no one, but the phrase struck a nerve: it got more ink in the press the next day than anything else in his speech, and it is still frequently quoted.

Following Bush's statement, more than one commentator advocated the development of a twelve-step program to rid America of its addiction to petroleum. The original twelve-step program of Alcoholics Anonymous was religion-based, so it might not be directly useful to an entire modern semi-secular society. But two of the steps could well apply:

- admitting that we have a problem, and
- making a searching and fearless inventory of our energy consumption.

In what other ways can the addiction metaphor be helpful? In his article "Is Our Collective Oil Dependence an Addiction?", Peak Oil activist Rob Hopkins concluded that dependency is a better metaphor than addiction in the current instance.[6] Hopkins cites the WHO diagnostic definition of dependency, which says that "three or more of the following manifestations should have occurred together for at least one month or, if persisting for periods of less than one month, should have occurred together repeatedly within a 12-month period":

- a strong desire or sense of compulsion to take the substance
- impaired capacity to control substance-taking behavior in terms of its onset, termination, or levels of use, as evidenced by: the

substance being often taken in larger amounts or over a longer
period than intended or by a persistent desire or unsuccessful efforts to reduce or control substance use

- a physiological withdrawal state when substance use is reduced
  or ceased, as evidenced by the characteristic withdrawal syn-
  drome for the substance, or by use of the same (or closely related) substance with the intention of relieving or avoiding
  withdrawal symptoms
- evidence of tolerance to the effects of the substance, such that
  there is a need for significantly increased amounts of the substance to achieve intoxication or the desired effect, or a markedly
  diminished effect with continued use of the same amount of the
  substance
- preoccupation with substance use, as manifested by important
  alternative pleasures or interests being given up or reduced because of substance use; or a great deal of time being spent in activities necessary to obtain, take, or recover from the effects of
  the substance
- persistent substance use despite clear evidence of harmful consequences, as evidenced by continued use when the individual is
  actually aware, or may be expected to be aware, of the nature
  and extent of harm[7]

Hopkins examines our societal dependence on oil in terms of each
of these criteria and makes the case that each applies.

If we accept that the metaphor does have value and that society
is, in some sense, clinically dependent upon a damaging substance
(oil), what implications does this have for public policy?

Let us suppose that we genuinely wished to end our dependency
on some other damaging substance, such as heroin. How would we
go about doing this? One method might be to surround ourselves
with methadone, cigarettes, beer, coffee, and chewing gum — that
is, with other addictive or habit-forming substances — and then
hope that our dependency on heroin somehow transferred itself to
one or more of these. The strategy would probably not work well;
the more likely outcome would be at least one *added* dependency.

Let us translate this thought exercise to our oil dependency. Might we end it simply by developing new supplies of alternative fuels such as ethanol and biodiesel, or liquids from coal and natural gas? If the analogy holds, the result is likely to be not an actual *re-duction* in oil consumption but merely an *added* dependency on these alternatives. And indeed this is exactly what we see in most cases: it is difficult to find an instance in which any nation has sub-stantially decreased its existing oil consumption as a result of the de-velopment of alternative fuels. In nearly every case alternatives serve merely to reduce *the rate of growth* in demand for oil. It doesn't hurt, but neither does it address the core problem.

For the typical heroin user, a reduction in consumption can only be accomplished by dealing head-on with the dependency. Other habit-forming substances only serve as crutches after the fact. Simi-larly, the only way any modern nation like the US is likely to accom-plish President Bush's desire to "wean ourselves off of petroleum" and thus end its dependence on oil is to deliberately and systemati-cally reduce production and/or imports. This, of course, is pre-cisely the aim and consequence of the Oil Depletion Protocol, the subject of my previous book.

Proactive Application: Social Marketing

Psychology has its non-therapeutic, even mercenary uses, which have not gone unnoticed by various armies and intelligence serv-ices, nor by corporate marketeers. The former, in the old USSR, Nazi Germany, and China, as well as the US, developed several psychologically devastating techniques for interrogation and brain-washing. Recent revelations about interrogation techniques em-ployed by American soldiers and CIA agents at the Abu Ghraib prison in Iraq show that such methods are still being refined and ap-plied. Publicly released records of psychological experiments by CIA scientists go back at least to the 1950s; techniques include the administration of hallucinogenic drugs, sleep deprivation, long-term pain infliction, and humiliation, among others.

The advertising and public relations industries have used psy-chology to less overtly cruel but equally manipulative ends. Their

Sigmund Freud. Credit: Public Domain

efforts to develop methods for shaping tastes and opinions, and changing mass behavior, date back to the early decades of the last century. The story of one individual, Edward Bernays (1891–1995), is worth relating very briefly in this regard. Bernays literally wrote the book on *Propaganda* (the title of his 1928 *magnum opus*), and his achievements were admired and imitated by Goebbels. Bernays was, as he never tired of pointing out, Sigmund Freud's nephew, and he energetically adapted his uncle's findings — along with those of Ivan Pavlov — to the seemingly mundane purposes of selling products and making companies look good. Bernays's clients included General Motors, Procter & Gamble, CBS, the American Tobacco Company, and General Electric. He is today commonly regarded as one of the pioneers of the modern public relations industry, but contemporary political strategists like Karl Rove also owe him a debt of gratitude.

While the efforts of Bernays and his heirs have highly questionable value for enhancing the survival potential of our species, if humanity is to adapt successfully and proactively to the twin threats of Peak Oil and climate chaos then mass behavior change will be needed. The public's strenuous efforts will have to be enlisted. Some knowledge of psychology could be used, not to extract information or sell merchandise and political candidates, but to help the populace understand its plight and adapt its behavior to post-hydrocarbon existence.

A relatively new field known as social marketing is directly relevant to our needs and purposes in this regard; its goal is mass behavior change that is in the public's own interest. Perhaps the best introduction to the subject is the book *Fostering Sustainable Behav-*

ior by Doug MacKenzie-Mohr and William Smith.[8] A few of its relevant findings are worth mentioning.

According to MacKenzie-Mohr and Smith, information by itself rarely is sufficient to inspire people to change their behavior. In the present context, that means that just telling the world about Peak Oil or Climate Change will not immediately cause millions or billions of people to replace their cars with bicycles. In order to be motivated, most people need to see new behavior modeled by others whom they admire or respect. They respond better to messages

Edward Bernays (1891–1995), Freud's nephew and one of the founders of the public relations industry. Credit: Public Domain

from community members — neighbors — than those from distant experts. The first task of people wishing to foster new sustainable behaviors, according to the authors, must be to identify barriers to those behaviors (perhaps through focus groups or other research), and to find practical, acceptable ways to circumvent them.

Many of the examples in the book have to do with promoting recycling programs. Of course, the behavior changes that will be required in the next decades will be on a different scale altogether, and the barriers will be many and deep. Moreover, social marketing, if it is to accomplish much in this context, will have to overcome a tremendous tide of messages running in the opposite direction — i.e., the pied-piper tune of the advertisers telling one and all to buy and consume more stuff, and seeking to convince us that the consumptive party is only just beginning. Can social marketers, with their typically minuscule budgets, hope to parry this cheerier and far more formidably financed message with one asking for what amounts to personal sacrifice of convenience and comfort?

In my view, social marketing could only be of much help if it were applied on a scale far beyond anything discussed in *Fostering Sustainable Behavior.* We will need Washington, Hollywood, Madison Avenue, Main Street, and Wall Street all on board delivering a coordinated message to both the elites and the masses — as was the case during World War II. We will need the kind of cooperative effort that Cuba mustered during its Special Period, when collective survival required a rapid, systemic reform of the nation's food and transport systems. But how can collective work on such a scale be commandeered in peacetime, and in democratic, free-market societies?

This is no small problem. Advertisers, manufacturers, politicians, economists, and the general public will all have to grow some wisdom, and do so quickly to override customary impulses toward individualism and the preservation of familiar comforts.

Rob Hopkins and Robert Hirsch have both spoken of our need for mobilization regarding Peak Oil and Climate Change as being on the same scale as the Second World War. The evidence plainly shows that the threat to our collective survival presented by Peak Oil and Climate Change today is greater than that posed by the Axis powers during the 1940s. If ever in the past a heroic collective effort was called for, it is needed even more now.

Do I think it's going to happen? Frankly, it's not likely. Is it possible in principle? Yes, just barely. As long as there is life and breath, we should be working toward that end. If nothing else, we'll feel better about ourselves and about life in general if we at least try.

8

Bridging Peak Oil and Climate Change Activism

T HE PROBLEMS OF Climate Change and Peak Oil both result from societal dependence on fossil fuels. But just how the impacts of these two problems relate to one another, and how policies to address them should differ or overlap, are questions that have so far not been adequately discussed.

Despite the fact that they are closely related, the two issues are in many respects dissimilar. Climate Change has to do with carbon emissions and their effects — including the impacts on human societies from rising sea levels, widespread and prolonged droughts, habitat loss, extreme weather events, and so on. Peak Oil, on the other hand, has to do with coming shortfalls in the supply of fuels on which society has become overwhelmingly dependent — leading, certainly, to higher prices for oil and its many byproducts, and perhaps to massive economic disruption and more oil wars. Thus the first has more directly to do with the environment, the second with human society and its dependencies and vulnerabilities. At the most superficial level, we could say that Climate Change is an end-of-tailpipe problem, while Peak Oil is an into-fuel-tank problem.

Because of this crucial divergence, the training and priorities of people who study one problem often differ from those of people who study the other. Most advocates for the Peak Oil concept — sometimes known as "depletionists" — are energy experts, economists, journalists, urban planners, or workers retired from the oil industry (usually geologists or petroleum engineers). Among climate analysts and activists there are more environmentalists, fewer energy experts, and far fewer retired oil industry employees. It is my experience that, when placed in the same room together, the two groups often talk past one another.

My own background is primarily as an environmentalist: I teach a college course on human ecology and have been writing about ecological issues for 15 years or so; at the same time, I find myself identified primarily as a Peak Oil activist, having written three books about the subject and having given something like 300 lectures on it. To me, head-butting arguments between the two groups as to which problem is more serious constitute a peculiar kind of hell, in that such arguments can only hamper the efforts of both groups to do what we all agree is essential — avert environmental and human catastrophe. Nevertheless, disagreements and misunderstandings are already emerging for the simple reason that advocates on both issues are competing to persuade the public of the central importance of their own cause.

Since such competitive disagreements are ultimately damaging to our broader collective interests, it seems important to devote some effort toward openly discussing the differences and similarities of the issues themselves, as well as the priorities and views of their respective advocates. This essay is intended to be exploratory and descriptive rather than polemic; my assumption is that it is better for the issues to be clarified and discussed than for them to remain unarticulated. My thesis is that both groups are essentially working toward a reduction in society's consumption of fossil fuels, and that cooperative efforts between the two groups could substantially strengthen their arguments and their effectiveness at persuading policymakers.

Differing Perspectives

While the Peak Oil and Climate Change issues may themselves be relatively clear and discrete, the groups of scientists and activists who study and organize around them are far from being internally homogeneous. Some individuals and groups working on issues related to oil and natural gas depletion are well informed about climate science, while some are not. Some climate protection groups are sensitive to fuel-supply vulnerability issues; others are not. Some Peak Oil activists are what have come to be known in the blog world as "doomers" — they believe that there is no hope for the preservation of modern civilization in any recognizable form; others are "techno-fixers," who think that the world will adjust to oil depletion — painfully perhaps, but in the end successfully — through conservation and the development of alternative energy sources. Similarly there are "moderate" Climate Change scientists and activists who see the problem as serious but solvable, while

This photo, taken by Wing-Chi Poon on 4th July 2005 at the tip of Athabasca Glacier, Jasper National Park, Alberta, Canada, shows a river of melt-water running down the slope of a toe of the Glacier. Globally, virtually all glaciers are in retreat. This implies future fresh water shortages for hundreds of millions or billions of people in regions (including Ecuador, Peru, Bolivia, and the Himalayas) that rely on glacier melt-water during summer months. Credit: Wing-Chi Poon

there are some who believe that the world has already passed the tipping point beyond which catastrophic impacts are inevitable. It is probably fair to say that the substantial majority of both groups find themselves somewhere midway between the extreme positions staked out by some of their spokespeople.

So, given this lack of homogeneity within the groups, it would be inappropriate to generalize too much and I will try as best I can to remain sensitive to these differences and overlaps during the following discussion. After giving some thought to the matter, I have chosen not to mention names of individuals who hold the views that I will be describing.

Let us begin with the group I know better — the depletionists. It is fair to note that some Peak Oil analysts seem to be of the opinion that oil depletion constitutes a solution to the dilemma of global greenhouse gas emissions, or that Climate Change is actually not a problem at all. This appears to be the view primarily of some former oil industry geologists, but is probably not that of the majority of depletion analysts. The view is rarely stated openly (I was unable to find a glaring instance in print, though I have heard it expressed in conversation). Nevertheless, it is a notion that understandably causes concern and consternation among Climate Change activists.

For their part, many Climate Change activists and experts see global warming as potentially having such devastating consequences, not just for humans but for the whole biosphere, that Peak Oil seems a trivial concern by comparison. They argue that even if global oil production peaks soon, this will provide no solution whatever to Climate Change because society will replace oil with

As arctic ice melts, it leaves much darker open water, which absorbs more heat from sunlight, causing yet more ice to melt — a reinforcing feedback loop. It is now projected that the northern polar region will be free of ice during the summer months within three or four decades. Credit: National Oceanic and Atmospheric Administration

coal and other low-grade fossil fuels, which will simply increase greenhouse gas emissions. Moreover, since the remedies for carbon emissions that climate activists propose will inevitably lead to increased energy efficiency and a reduction in oil consumption, they often feel such efforts constitute an adequate answer to the Peak Oil problem.

Most oil depletionists (excepting the small group discussed above) appear to hold the opinion that Climate Change is indeed a legitimate concern; however, since the economic impact of Peak Oil looms in the immediate future, the economic and geopolitical chaos that may be triggered by declining global fuel supplies pose the more urgent threat. Some have argued that if Peak Oil results in near-term economic collapse and wars over dwindling energy resources, these events will seriously or terminally undermine the ability of national leaders to undertake the cooperative, long-range planning necessary to reduce carbon emissions.

For many Climate Change activists, theirs is primarily a moral issue having to do with the fate of future generations and other species. Their message implies an appeal to self-preservation, but since they cannot prove that the most horrific climate consequences being predicted (the drowning of coastal cities by rising seas, rapidly expanding deserts, collapsing agricultural production) will occur within the next decade or two, the motive of self-preservation is often downplayed. This emphasis on the moral dimension of climate activism is clear in Al Gore's documentary film, *An Inconvenient Truth*.

It is probably safe to say that most Peak Oil activists are motivated more by their immediate concerns for preservation of self, family, and community. They see the peak of global oil production as happening soon and the effects accumulating quickly. This concern for self-preservation is prominent in the quasi-survivalist tone of several Peak Oil websites.

Climate Change activists see the argument that depletion will take care of the carbon emissions problem as a threat, because it could lead to apathy. They argue that there are enough fossil fuels left on the planet to trigger a climatic doomsday and, to underscore the argument, Climate Change activists often quote robust estimates of remaining oil reserves and amounts awaiting discovery issued by agencies such as the United States Energy Information Administration (EIA), and by companies like ExxonMobil and Cambridge Energy Research Associates (CERA) — which seem unrealistically optimistic compared to the majority of expert forecasts. Climate activists understandably feel fully justified in doing this, because, after all, these are *official* estimates and forecasts.

Peak Oil activists adhere to more pessimistic resource estimates and production forecasts, and it is tempting to think that this is partly because doing so makes their case appear stronger. However, the track record of prediction by the optimists is not good:

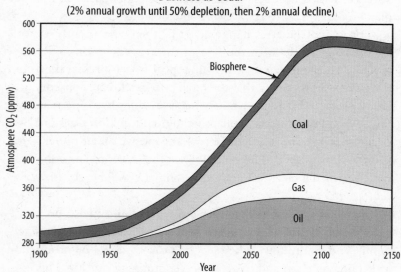

Business as Usual
(2% annual growth until 50% depletion, then 2% annual decline)

Figure 19. Atmospheric CO_2 concentrations by source. This assumes no voluntary cuts in emissions — hence "business as usual." Hansen assumes Peak Oil and Gas will not happen for 20 years, and that there will be no peak for coal until after 2100. In this case, the greenhouse gas contribution from oil and natural gas will be much less significant than that from coal. However, compare this chart with Figure 2 in the Introduction. Credit: James Hansen, NASA

- During the 1960s, the US Geological Survey issued successive reports forecasting a peak in US oil production around the year 2000; this followed M. King Hubbert's controversial forecast of a peak around the year 1970. Confounding the official view, US oil production did reach its maximum in 1970 and has been generally declining ever since, despite the subsequent discovery of the largest conventional oilfield ever found in North America, on the North Slope of Alaska in the 1970s.
- In their International Energy Outlook (IEO) 2001 report, the EIA stated that "the United Kingdom is expected to produce about 3.1 mb/d by the middle of this decade, followed by a decline to 2.7 mb/d by 2020," implying a peak around 2005.

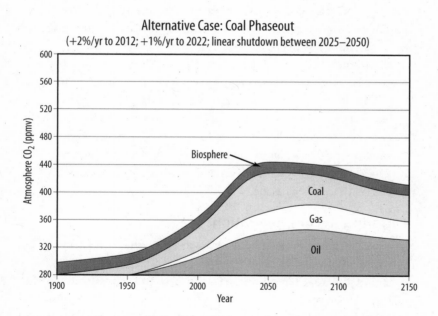

Alternative Case: Coal Phaseout
(+2%/yr to 2012; +1%/yr to 2022; linear shutdown between 2025–2050)

Figure 20. Atmospheric concentrations of greenhouse gases by source, constrained model. In this chart, Hansen assumes voluntary cuts in GHG emissions from coal, with 2 percent per year growth until 2012 followed by sequestration of CO2 at new coal power plants, the mothballing of inefficient non-sequestering coal power plants in the period from 2025 to 2050, the avoidance of non-conventional fossil fuels, and curtailing of growth in use of oil and gas through a slowly increasing carbon tax. Credit: James Hansen, NASA.

Britain's oil production from the North Sea actually peaked in 1999, two years *before* this forecast was issued, at 2.684 mb/d, declining to less than 1.7 mb/d by 2005.

- In their IEO 2003 report, the EIA predicted that the country of Oman was "expected to increase output gradually over the first half of this decade" with "only a gradual production decline after 2005." In fact, Oman's production had already peaked in 2000, three years before the forecast was published.

This pattern of unrealistic optimism on the part of the official forecasting agencies has continued with regard to other countries, and thus probably, by extrapolation, to their forecasts for the world as a whole. So it might be unrealistic for the climate activists to give credence to such forecasts, or even to assume that the truth lies equidistant between the extreme resource estimates of the so-called optimists and pessimists.

Parenthetically, both Peak Oil and Climate Change activists have reasons (though different ones) to regard ExxonMobil as an arch-foe. That company has consistently funded groups undermining public concern about Climate Change. And recently ExxonMobil has placed prominent magazine ads proclaiming that the global oil production peak is so far in the future that we need not worry about it. One ExxonMobil executive has been widely quoted as saying, "Peak oil theory is garbage."

Differing Recommendations

These differences in perspective lead to somewhat divergent policy recommendations.

For Climate Change analysts and activists, emissions are the essence of the problem, and so anything that will reduce emissions is viewed as a solution. If societies shift from using a high-carbon fossil fuel (coal) to a fuel with lower carbon content (natural gas), this is an obvious benefit in terms of climate risk — and a potentially easy sell to politicians and the general public, because it merely requires a change of fuel, not a sacrifice of convenience or comfort. And so, again, climate analysts tend to accept at face value official high reserves estimates and production forecasts — in this case, for natural gas.

However, as with oil, production forecasts by the official agencies for natural gas supply have tended to be overly robust. For example, in the US the EIA issued no warning whatever of future domestic natural gas problems prior to the supply shortfalls that became painfully apparent after 2000, as prices more than quadrupled. Nevertheless, a few industry insiders had noted disturbing signs: companies were drilling at an accelerating pace in order to maintain production rates, and newer fields (which tended to be smaller) were depleting ever more quickly. By 2003 the US Energy Secretary was proclaiming a natural gas crisis. In the following three years, warm weather (perhaps due to Climate Change) and demand reduction (from the off-shoring of many industrial users of natural gas due to high domestic prices) led to a partial relaxing of prices and general complacency. However, US domestic production appears set to decline further, and likely at a rapid pace.

For depletion analysts and activists, societal dependence on vanishing, non-renewable energy resources is the essence of the greatest dilemma that our society currently faces. We have created a complex, global economic infrastructure built to run on fuels that will start to become scarce and expensive very soon. From this perspective, natural gas is not a solution but an enormous problem: even if the global peak in gas production is 10 to 20 years away, regional shortages are already appearing and will continue to intensify. This means enormous risks for home heating, for the chemicals and plastics industries, and for electrical power generation. Natural gas is and will always be a fuel that is, for the most part, regionally traded (as opposed to liquid fuels, which are more easily shipped). Thus for many nations critical to the world economy — the US, Britain, and most of continental Europe — gas cannot serve as a "transition fuel."

Coal presents another controversial topic for both depletion and emissions analysts. Most members of both groups feel a keen need to articulate some politically palatable transition strategy so as to gain the ears of policy makers. If coal were entirely ruled out of the discussion, such a strategy would become more difficult to cobble together. However, the two groups tend to think of very different future roles for coal.

Some emissions activists and analysts look to "clean coal" as a partial solution to the problem of Climate Change. "Clean coal" practices include gasifying coal underground, *in situ,* separating the resulting greenhouse gases (carbon dioxide and carbon monoxide), and then burying these in ocean sediments or old oilfields or coal-mines. This theoretically allows society to gain an energy benefit while reducing additions to atmospheric greenhouse gases.

Many depletion analysts are skeptical of such "carbon capture" schemes, believing that when the world is mired in a supply-driven energy crisis, few nations will be adequately motivated to pay the extra cost (in both financial and energy terms) to separate, handle, and store the carbon from coal; instead they will simply burn whatever is available in order to keep their economies from crashing.

Some depletionists see the world's enormous coal reserves as a partial supply-side answer to Peak Oil. Using a time-proven process, it is possible to gasify coal and then use the resulting gases to synthesize a high-quality diesel fuel. The South African company Sasol, which has updated the process, is currently under contract to provide several new coal-to-liquids (CTL) plants to China and has announced a plant in Montana.

CTL is not attractive to emissions analysts, however. While some carbon could be captured during the gasification stage (at a modest energy cost), burning the final liquid fuel would release as much carbon into the atmosphere as would burning conventional petroleum diesel.

A few depletion analysts tend to take a skeptical view of future coal supplies. According to most widely-quoted estimates, the world has one to two hundred years' worth of coal — at current rates of usage. However, factoring in dramatic increases in usage (to substitute for declining oil and gas supplies), while also taking account of the Hubbert peak phenomenon — extraction rates will inevitably begin to decline long before the coal actually runs out — and the fact that coal resources are of varying quality and accessibility leads to the surprising conclusion that a global peak in coal production could arrive as soon as a decade from now.[1] That raises the question: does it make sense to place great hope in largely untested and expensive carbon sequestration technologies if the new infrastructure needed will be nearly obsolete so soon? Imagine the world investing trillions of dollars and working mightily for the next 20 years to build hundreds of "clean" coal (and/or CTL) plants, with the world's electrical grids and transportation systems now becoming overwhelmingly dependent on these technologies, only to see global coal supplies dwindle. Would the world then have the capital to engage in *another* strenuous and costly energy transition? And what would be the next energy source?

Other low-grade fossil fuels, such as tar sands, oil shale, and heavy oil are also problematic from both the depletion and emissions perspectives. Some depletion analysts recommend full-speed development of these resources. However, the energetic extraction costs for them are usually quite high compared to the energy payoff from the resource extracted. Their already-low energy profit ratio (also known as the energy returned on energy invested, or EROEI) would be compromised still further by efforts to capture and sequester carbon, since, as with coal, these low-grade fuels have a high carbon content as compared to natural gas or conventional oil. Currently, natural gas is used in the processing of tar sands and heavy oil; from both an energy and an emissions point of view, this is rather like turning gold into lead. Many depletionists point out that, while the total resource base for these substances is enormous, the rate of extraction for each is likely to remain limited by physical factors (such as the availability of natural gas and fresh water needed for processing), so that synthetic liquid fuels from such substances may not help much in dealing with the problem of oil depletion in any case.

Supply Side, Demand Side

By now a disturbing trend becomes clear: the two problems of Climate Change and Peak Oil together are worse than either by itself. Strategies that are proposed to keep lights burning and trucks moving while reducing emissions are questionable from a depletionist point of view, while most strategies to keep the economy energized as oil and gas disappear imply increasing greenhouse gas emissions. As we will see, the closer we look, the worse it gets.

As noted above, both groups need to design a survivable energy transition strategy in order to sell their message to policy makers. Carbon emissions come from burning depleting fossil fuels, the primary energy source for modern societies. Thus both problems boil down to energy problems — and energy is essential to the maintenance of agriculture, transportation, communication, and just about everything else that makes up the modern global economy.

With regard to both problems there are only two kinds of solutions: substitution strategies (finding replacement energy sources) and conservation strategies (using energy more efficiently or just doing without). The former are politically preferable, as they do not require behavioral change or sacrifice, though they tend to require more planning and investment. The least palatable option, from a political standpoint, is also the quickest and cheapest — doing without (curtailing current usage). We have gotten used to using enormous amounts of energy at unprecedented rates. If we had to use much less, could we maintain the levels of comfort and economic growth that we have become accustomed to? Could we even keep the lights on?

Several questions become critical: How much of a reduction in energy supply will be imposed by the peaking of production of oil, natural gas, and coal? How much will be required in order to minimize Climate Change? And how much of that supply shortfall can be made up for with substitution and how much with efficiency, before we have to resort to curtailment?

Climate analysts agree the world needs to reduce emissions considerably. In 1996 the European Environment Council said that the global average surface temperature increase should be capped at a maximum of two degrees Celsius above pre-industrial levels, and that to accomplish this the atmospheric concentration of carbon dioxide (CO_2) will have to be stabilized at 550 parts per million (the current concentration is 380 ppm, though the addition of other greenhouse gases raises the figure to the equivalent of 440 to 450 ppm of CO_2). But recent studies have tended to suggest that, in order to achieve the two degree cap, much lower CO_2 levels will be needed. One study by researchers at the Potsdam Institute for Climate Impact in Germany concluded that — again, to keep the temperature from increasing more than two degrees Celsius — the atmospheric concentration target should be 440 ppm of CO_2 equivalents, implying that the atmospheric concentration of greenhouse gases will need to be stabilized at current levels. But, to make the challenge even more difficult, it turns out that the biosphere's ability to absorb carbon is being reduced by human activity, and this must be factored into the equation; by 2030, this carbon-absorbing ability will have been reduced from the current 4 billion tons per year to 2.7 billion. Thus if an equilibrium level of atmospheric carbon is to be maintained through 2030, emissions will have to be *reduced* from the current annual level of 7 billion tons to 2.7 billion tons, a reduction of 60 percent. It is hard to imagine how, if that translated to a 60 percent reduction in *energy consumption*, it could mean anything but economic ruin for the world.

Depletion analysts look to about a two percent per year decline in oil extraction following the peak of global oil production, with the rate increasing somewhat as time goes on. Coal extraction, following the production peak, will probably decline more slowly, at least for the first decades. Regional natural gas decline rates will be much steeper. The dates for global production peaks for these fuels are of course still a matter for speculation; however, it is reasonable to estimate that we might see a 25 to 45 percent decline in energy available to the world's growing population over the next quarter-century as a result of depletion.

Everyone would be happy if it were possible simply to substitute renewable sources of energy for oil, coal, and gas, and both depletion activists and climate activists support the expansion of most renewable energy technologies, including solar and wind. But there are realistic limits to the scale at which renewables can be deployed, and to the speed with which this can be accomplished.

Not all depletion or emissions activists support the large-scale development of biofuels (ethanol, butanol, and biodiesel), which are the only realistic renewable replacements for liquid transport fuels, because of the low EROEI entailed in making these fuels, and because these substitutes imply worrisome tradeoffs with food production.

Some depletionists and some climate analysts recommend expanding nuclear power, arguing that technological advances could make it a safe and affordable alternative. Others argue against it, noting that high-grade ores will be depleted in 60 years, and that the entire nuclear cycle of mining, refining, enrichment, plant construction, and so on (excluding fission itself) is carbon intensive. One analysis suggests that, from the mid-2020s, the task of clearing up all past and future nuclear wastes will require more energy than the industry can generate from the remaining ore.[2]

Then comes the equity issue. A few nations have benefited disproportionately from fossil fuels. If "developing" nations that have not yet had that opportunity are now required to forgo it, they will understandably perceive this as grossly unfair. They are unlikely to agree to dramatically reduce their own carbon emissions (i.e., fossil fuel consumption) unless already-industrialized nations lead the way and reduce theirs proportionally more. Also, it's necessary that at least a few of the "developing" nations — the ones that are rapidly industrializing now — be brought on board any global emissions or depletion agreement for it to have real meaning, as they have the economies with the fastest growth in energy demand. The prime example: while for practical purposes Americans will probably continue to lead the world in *per capita* fossil fuel use for some time, China has overtaken the US as the world's foremost national emitter of greenhouse gases.

Theoretically, the fairest solution, from an emissions point of view, would be to assign each living human an equal per capita right to emit carbon, and to create a market for those rights, so that continued disproportionate fossil fuel consumption by already-industrialized nations would entail substantial payments to less-industrialized nations. Fairness would also imply a steeper rate of reduction in fossil fuel consumption by the heavier users — a cut in emissions of considerably more than 60 percent.

However, to ask industrialized nations to share their wealth with less-industrialized nations while the former are engaged in a partially self-imposed energy famine seems highly problematic. What politician could demand the extra sacrifice? What public would vote for such a policy?

Where does this leave us? Let's assume that the more pessimistic critical analyses of both groups are correct. That is, let's say that a 60 percent reduction in emissions is needed within 25 years, that natural gas will not be available in sufficient quantities to serve as a transition fuel, that "clean" coal will not help much, that low-grade fossil fuels will not make up for shortfalls in oil production, that CTL production will remain marginal, that renewables will not come on line in sufficient quantity or soon enough, that nuclear power won't come to the rescue — and that modest contributions from these sources *added together* will not come close to making up for shortfalls from oil, gas, and coal depletion or from the voluntary phasing out of carbon fuels.

If this turns out to be the case, we may face a staggering need for energy efficiency and curtailment. Neither group wants this as its political platform.

Common Ground

As we have seen, there are understandable reasons for some climate activists to ignore the arguments and priorities of depletionists, and vice versa. Dealing with only one of the two problems is much easier than confronting both. But our goal must be to deal with reality, rather than merely our preferred image of reality, and reality is complicated. Our world faces the interacting impacts not only of Peak Oil and Climate Change, but also of water scarcity, overpopulation, over-fishing, chemical pollution, and war (among others). In the end, there are too many of us using too much too fast, while competing for dwindling resources.

What would it take to solve all of these problems at once? A good start would be to require a global across-the-board 2 to 5 percent per year reduction in fossil fuel consumption and the provision of substantial financial and technical aid by industrialized nations to less-industrialized nations in creating as much of a renewable energy infrastructure as is possible. But to the patient (the main fossil fuel users) this medicine might seem worse than the disease. A grand plan like this has almost no chance of gaining political backing.

Realistically, we are left with the customary policy tools meant to ameliorate the world's ills piecemeal: emissions and depletion protocols, tradeable quotas, emissions rights, import and export quotas, carbon taxes, and cap-and-trade mechanisms.

Thus for practical reasons it is probably inevitable that, to a certain extent at least, emissions and depletion activists will continue to pursue their separate policy goals. But it makes sense for the two groups to be informed by one another, and to cooperate wherever possible.

It is fairly obvious why such cooperation would benefit the depletionists: Climate Change is already a subject of considerable international concern and action, whereas Peak Oil is still a relatively new topic of discussion. This is partly because Climate Change fits well with the environmentalists' previous pollution-centred campaigns.

But how would such cooperation aid emissions activists?

In a word: motivation. As discussed earlier, emissions activists appeal to an ethical impulse to avert future harm to the environment and human society, while the Peak Oil issue appeals to a more immediate concern for self-preservation. In extreme circumstances, the latter is unquestionably the stronger motive. Strong motivation will certainly be required in order for the people of the world to undertake the enormous personal and social sacrifices required in order to quickly and dramatically reduce their fossil fuel dependency. Sustainability and equity are issues that are hard enough to campaign on in times of prosperity; when families and nations are struggling to maintain themselves due to fuel shortages and soaring prices, only massive education and persuasion campaigns could possibly summon the needed support.

Taken together, Climate Change and Peak Oil make a nearly airtight argument. We *should* reduce our dependency on fossil fuels for the sake of future generations and the rest of the biosphere; but even if we choose not to do so because of the costs involved, those fossil fuels will soon become more scarce and expensive anyway, so complacency is simply not an option.

What would cooperation between the two groups look like? It would help, first of all, for activists on one issue to spend more time studying the literature of the other, and for both groups to arrange meetings and conferences where the intersections of the two issues can be further explored.

Both groups could work together more explicitly to promote proactive, policy-driven reductions in fossil fuel consumption.

Climate activists could start using depletion arguments and data in tandem with their ongoing discussions of ice cores and melting glaciers, but to do so they would need to stop taking unrealistically robust resource estimates at face value.

For their part, depletionists — if they are to take advantage of increased collaboration with emissions activists — must better familiarize themselves with climate science, so that their Peak Oil mitigation proposals lead to a reduction rather than an increase of carbon emissions into the atmosphere.

Perhaps, for both groups, with a stronger potential for motivating the public will come the courage to tell a truth that few policy makers want to hear: energy efficiency and curtailment will almost certainly have to be the world's dominant responses to both issues.

9

Boomers' Last Chance?

IN HIS BEST-SELLING 1998 book *The Greatest Generation,*
Tom Brokaw extolled the virtues of the American women and
men, now deep into their retirement years, who grew up during the
Great Depression and fought in World War II. Brokaw's book con-
trasted "the greatest generation any society ever produced" with
those that preceded and followed it. The cohort born during World
War I and up to 1930 faced immense adversity and made sacrifices
that ensured the survival of freedom and democracy; as a result,
their children have enjoyed the most extended and exuberant period of affluence in the history of any nation.

Brokaw and I are children of that generation; ours is the so-
called Baby Boom demographic cohort, about which an oil tanker's
worth of ink has been spilled in self-adulation, self-criticism, self-
analysis, and general self-obsession. I hesitate to join in the orgy of
generational mirror gazing, but I can't help but reflect on a simple
fact: during my lifetime, and that of my cohort, about half of the
non-renewable resources of the planet will have been used. Gone,
forever.

This is a generation that has practiced diachronic competition
(that is, competition with *future* generations) more ruthlessly than
any other since the dawn of our species. The implications are devastating.

I might dispute Brokaw's assertion that the World War II generation was the best in history (in fact I will do so below); nevertheless, a good case could be made that my generation, because it so
threatens the perpetuation of its kind and the survival of countless
other species, is the *worst* ever.

Mea culpa.

Of course, in a way the very idea of a "generation" is arbitrary.
The notion implies discreteness where there is continuity. Worse
still, discussion of "better" or "worse" generations entails a moral
judgment where one is not called for, by assuming that all of the
members of a demographic cohort somehow deserve equal praise
or blame, when in fact this is never the case. It may make sense to
speak of the moral triumphs or failures of individuals, but the application of such judgments to whole generations is problematic.

However there is one respect in which the discussion has merit:
much of Brokaw's argument revolves around the truism that a demographic cohort is shaped by historical circumstances. Individuals
within that cohort inevitably respond to events differently one from
another and help shape subsequent history in divergent ways, yet
members of each generation undeniably share a certain commonal-
ity of experience — notably so during periods of large-scale, dramatic change.

Brokaw's "greatest generation" was tempered by adversity. In
contrast, the Boomers have been spoiled by abundance. In the US,
one generation presided over that nation's ascendancy while the
other is overseeing its peak in power and wealth and the beginning
of its inevitable decline. The post-World War II generation in many
other nations has likewise enjoyed the brightest years of material
abundance, though there are certainly exceptions.

But if we follow the implications of this environmental deter-
minist view, then we have to conclude that the World War II generation was not so praiseworthy after all, nor are the Boomers so
uniformly culpable. All of us are mostly responding to circumstances beyond our control.

In this chapter I hope to explore some of the circumstances that
have made us Boomers what and who we are, and to argue that,

having failed to live up to some of our expressed ideals and now finding ourselves in power just as the industrial world is beginning its decline, we may have one last opportunity to redeem ourselves.

What Made the "Greatest Generation" Great

Brokaw's book was in some respects a peace offering — an attempt to close the generation gap that opened up in the 1960s as young people wrangled with their parents over drugs, sex, music, hairstyles, and the Vietnam War. Steven Spielberg's *Saving Private Ryan* was another bouquet thrown from the younger (now aging) generation to its elders. The message implicit in both: We, the Boomers, appreciate and respect our parents' sacrifices and hard work, which made it possible for us to enjoy the peace, freedom, and affluence that we have mostly taken for granted throughout our lives.

The bouquet is no doubt deserved in many individual instances. *The Greatest Generation* is filled with stories of undeniable heroism (though for more politically informed anecdotal reports of the experiences and contributions of the elder cohort see Studs Terkel's *Hard Times: An Oral History of the Great Depression,* published by Norton in 2000, and *The Good War: An Oral History of World War II,* released by New Press in 1997).

However, the freedom and affluence of modern Americans are due not just to courage and endurance but also sheer luck. Let us not forget that the people who inhabited the United States in the early 20th century happened to be sitting on one fabulous pile of natural resources — everything from forests, fresh water, fertile soils, and fish to minerals (gold, nickel, iron, aluminum, copper) to energy resources (oil, natural gas, coal, and uranium). Moreover, the US has enjoyed geographic isolation from Eurasian intrigues, which enabled it to thrive during occasions when Europeans and Asians were tearing each other to bits.

Thus the payoff that came at the end of World War II carried an historic inevitability: with its resource base, factories, and highly motivated work force, the US had helped win the war without damage to its internal infrastructure. In contrast, Britain and the USSR had also emerged winners, but only after seeing their cities, railroads, and factories bombed. While the rest of the industrial world lay in ruins, America stood unscathed.

Because of the American economy's stability, the US dollar was adopted as a reserve currency by other nations. American oil wells supplied over half the total amount of petroleum being extracted globally. Sixty percent of all export goods delivered throughout the world carried a "Made in USA" tag. General Motors was the world's biggest corporation and Hollywood films were on screens everywhere.

US factories made so many manufactured goods that Americans had to be cajoled into a permanent buying frenzy by the greatest propaganda system the world has ever seen — the American advertising industry — which made brilliant use of history's greatest propaganda medium — television. In fact, the consumerist project had gotten under way in the 1920s as fuel-fed American capitalism searched for solutions to the problem of over-production (a problem that was in fact one of the Depression's causes). But World War II's insatiable need for materiel and the post-war expansion of advertising and credit made the Depression vanish like a bad dream and sent the economy into warp drive. Indeed, in the 1950s human beings habitually came to be referred to not as "people" or "citizens" but "consumers."

Having lived through a decade when starving would-be employees competed for the few jobs available, people worked hard when finally given the chance. They saved. They believed in the American Dream and in the essential goodness of America's international leadership. They bought homes and raised families.

And that's where the Boomers come in.

The "Me" Generation

When people feel optimistic about the future and feel they will easily be able to support a large family they tend to have more children. And so, after the War's end, as soldiers came home and went to work building the suburban utopia, they sired the most numerous generational cohort America had ever seen. Demographers define baby-boomers as those born between 1946 and 1964 (as of 2007, members of the Boomer cohort are between 43 and 61 years of age). There are about 76 million US Boomers, representing a quarter of the population. And their tastes, lifestyles, and ambitions have transformed the nation — and to a large extent the world beyond — in a myriad of ways.

The "Father Knows Best" years in which the Boomers grew up were ones of unprecedented abundance and safety. Yes, there was a Cold War, there were a couple of recessions, and the last few of the Boomer cohort's formative years (from 1968 on) were tumultuous. But compare this quarter-century to any previous one in history: in Europe — one of the wealthiest regions of the planet — hardly a decade went by for centuries without a significant famine affecting an entire region. For Boomers the word *famine* held about as much personal relevance as Biblical verses about leprosy or marauding Philistines. No one in America actually *starved to death* — at least not in modern times, and certainly no one *we* knew did so. Far from it: Boomers knew only supermarkets filled with a numbing variety of cheap packaged or refrigerated foods, all conveniently accessed by way of automobiles (every family now had one) rolling serenely over smoothly paved streets and highways.

One measure of this new abundance was power available per capita. In the 19th century, most of the work being done in America was accomplished by means of animal or human muscle power. In 1850, fuel-fed machines supplied only about 18 percent of the total horsepower in the economy; the rest came from real horses, as well as oxen, mules, and human labor. Domestic servants were common. However, by 1960 machines were supplying virtually all of the power in the economy. People were still working, of course, and there were lots more of them (though by now there were far fewer working horses, and far fewer domestic servants), but their contribution had become inconsequential in terms of applied energy. Machines — and the fossil fuels that made them go — were supplying power for greatly expanded manufacturing, transportation, information storage and transmission, and so on. And so by the 1960s

Two hippies at Woodstock, August, 1969.
Credit: Paul Campbell

the typical American — even if his or her near ancestors had been slaves or servants — had access to as much power as that exerted by scores of laborers.

In short, Americans had every reason to believe that they were living in the best of all possible worlds, in the greatest of nations, in the best of times.

Why, then, the generation gap? Was there trouble in paradise?

Again: people are to some extent the product of the circumstances and events of their historical era. The younger generation, growing up in affluence, was free to take survival — even abundance — for granted. And we are discussing a level of abundance significantly greater, in some respects, even than exists today: at that time, the US was still solvent, still a net exporter of credit. In the 1960s an entire family could live on a single average income. Rents were cheap, land was cheap, and college was cheap.

Therefore rebellion was cheap, too. The young people knew they were different from their parents, and they could afford to question their parents' seeming obsession with discipline and hard work, their conformity and unflinching patriotism.

Meanwhile America was visibly and quickly changing: graceful old downtown buildings were collapsing under the wrecking ball while monotonous suburban housing developments and strip malls were sprouting where farmland used to be. America's wealth was being spent in a tasteless nouveau-riche spectacle designed by overpaid Madison Avenue huckster-bureaucrats in gray suits. The older generation was mostly proud of this transformation, but many young people couldn't help but notice the vapidity and emptiness of the corporate-sponsored theme-park way of life, and they had the free time to indulge in irony and sarcasm.

As Boomers went to college (a greater percentage of them did so than in any previous generation) they started asking questions, and the answers they found were troubling. They learned that the shining image of America the Free and Brave hid a history of slavery and genocide. Moreover, in their extracurricular reading they discovered that an increasing share of US wealth was emanating from an international imperial system enforced by the American military and the CIA.

This latter fact was driven home by the greatest single perception-shaping circumstance of the Boomers' young-adult lives — the Vietnam War. Pampered American teenagers were being called up, trained, and airlifted around the world to fight and die in a conflict they didn't understand. And an alarming number of them were coming home in pine boxes or body bags. Was this a heroic campaign against a malevolent foreign enemy bent on our destruction? Or was it an imperialist war of aggression against a Third-World nation led by a man widely regarded by his countrymen as the indigenous equivalent of George Washington? Disputes over the war divided families across America — my own included — and ran deep: for people on both sides of the debate what was at stake was nothing less than the essential character and future of the nation.

The Boomers' Defining Moments

Many of the happily memorable moments of the Boomer generation's early years are etched into the national psyche and have been recalled endlessly: teenage girls' shrieking response to the Beatles' first appearance on the Ed Sullivan Show; the Summer of Love in San Francisco in 1967; Grateful Dead concerts jammed with tripping, giddy hipsters; communes and head shops; Woodstock. But other images are more sobering and significant: the assassinations of JFK, RFK, and Martin Luther King, Jr.; the police riot at the 1968 Democratic Convention; the shootings at Kent State; the stirring to life of the Black Power movement, the American Indian Movement, the women's movement, and the Chicano/farm workers' movement; and the massive antiwar demonstrations that closed many colleges and universities in 1971.

However, the two events of that era that had the potential to

Rainbow gatherings, such as the one in Russia in 2005 where this photo was taken, keep the hippie ethos alive. Credit: Wikimedia, user alexkon

most profoundly shape the Boomers' lives, and those of their children, are less often dwelt on. Both occurred in 1970: the peak in US oil production and the first Earth Day.

At the time it happened, the US oil production peak went unnoticed; it was observed in hindsight a few years later, though even today it is scarcely mentioned in the press. One of the few who really understood its significance was the scientist who had anticipated it — geologist M. King Hubbert. Its consequences for the US economy and for global geopolitics would only gradually reveal themselves, with the first strong hint appearing in 1973's Arab oil embargo. Those consequences would eventually include the undermining of the entire American consumerist-imperialist project.

Of course oil was and is central to the automobile and airline industries, which have been major drivers of the US economy. Less obvious is oil's role in modern industrial agriculture. However, if one looks more deeply, the very fabric of 20th century America is petroleum-soaked. In 1900 the world's wealthiest and oiliest man was John D. Rockefeller, whose company, Standard Oil, had cornered the national market. Rockefeller himself was an abstemious churchgoer who believed that wealth was a sign of God's favor; what does such a person do with so much money? All sorts of things. Why not go into banking in order to make even more money? The Rockefeller family did so with a vengeance and was instrumental in creating the Federal Reserve System — the banking system that quietly controls the US currency and economy. If one is exceptionally wealthy it is also handy to have some influence over public opinion

— and so Rockefeller wealth found its way into controlling positions in media organizations. Even scientific research can have its uses: when I was tracing the history of genetic engineering for my 1999 book *Cloning the Buddha,* I discovered that the inception of molecular biology (the basis for all subsequent developments in genetic science) came in the 1920s as a result of strategic grants from the Rockefeller Foundation in its quest for a means of eugenic "social control." Politics, geopolitics, war, weapons manufacturing, education — all were deeply impacted by the Rockefeller oil fortune. Oil wasn't just a subsidy to American wealth; it formed the very substance and character of American wealth.

Therefore the fact that by 1971 US oil production had peaked and was in terminal decline was momentous (if unheralded) news. America could no longer be a *source* of wealth in the same way it had been; if it were to maintain its privileged position globally it would have to become the world's moneychanger, banker, landlord, stockbroker . . . and enforcer. American military force would have to be used increasingly to safeguard and protect US access to the resource wealth of *other* countries, while international trade agreements would have to be written and enforced to the advantage of American corporations. And those corporations would be ever less involved directly in manufacturing, but more in trading, branding, and licensing.

The other signal event of 1970 — the first Earth Day — was well noted at the time. The brainchild of Senator Gaylord Nelson, Earth Day was reported prominently in the *New York Times, Time,* and most other significant media outlets. Legislation followed: the National Environmental Policy Act, the Clean Air Act, the Water Quality Improvement Act, the Water Pollution and Control Act Amendments, the Resource Recovery Act,

The crowd at Woodstock filled a natural amphitheater, with the stage at the bottom. Credit: Paul Campbell.

the Resource Conservation and Recovery Act, the Toxic Substances Control Act, the Occupational Safety and Health Act, the Federal Environmental Pesticide Control Act, the Endangered Species Act, the Safe Drinking Water Act, the Federal Land Policy and Management Act, and the Surface Mining Control and Reclamation Act.

Perhaps even more important than this legislation was the symbolic value of the occasion in giving voice and identity to a growing minority who viewed the fossil-fueled industrial project as having dire consequences for humanity and nature, and who advocated a dramatic change of direction for society as a whole, away from consumerism and toward conservation, away from militarism and toward nurturance of life. The Earth Day message — which would be given renewed force two years later with the publication of the Club of Rome report, *The Limits to Growth*, and then again with the Arab oil embargo of 1973 — appealed to many young people's intuitive longing for a return to a simpler, more localized and agrarian version of America, an America that didn't meddle in other nations' affairs.

The Earth Day message might have been still more compelling had its framers been aware of the fact and significance of their nation's oil peak. However, though the message evoked legislative and cultural responses, it sank in only so deep. It was, after all, difficult for many Americans to accept the notion that they should voluntarily give up their material privileges, their control of global resource streams, their entitlement to a glittering technotopian future of effortless abundance, and accept instead a self-disciplined and self-limiting future of hard work and parsimonious material aspirations. The difficulty was compounded by the existence of an international rival, the USSR, that would presumably fill the void if America were to shrink from its imperial duties. The Soviet Union was also a competitor in the oil business and had actually out-produced the US in recent years. Wouldn't stepping off the consumerist treadmill mean giving in to the Commies?

It was a contest of visions and values, and that contest was to be decided in the election of 1980.

The Path Taken

Jimmy Carter was a less than perfect president; nevertheless, he somewhat understood the Earth Day message. I was living in Canada during the mid-1970s and almost never watched television, but I somehow found myself viewing the live broadcast of a Carter speech in which he told Americans that they would have to change their material way of life in order to keep their freedoms. I was so amazed to hear an American president saying such things that I moved back to the US. But the Carter years were destined to be few.

For over three decades the American Right had been searching for ways to overturn the New Deal. Corporate leaders backing the Republicans had managed to make common cause with the burgeoning Christian fundamentalist movement and the anti-Communist fringe; Nixon had perfected the strategy of bringing social conservatives from the old Confederacy into the Republican Party; and the party had found its perfect pitchman — a former movie actor and ex-spokesman for General Electric. Ronald Reagan and the Republican PR machine pushed all of the right buttons, even resorting to an "October surprise" to manipulate the Iranian hostage crisis to their benefit.

Reagan and George H. W. Bush (who, during the mid-1980s, may have been the de facto president) were the last US leaders of the World War II generation, their cohort's final gift to the nation. It was morning in America, but let the Earth be damned: the Republicans had found an electoral strategy so successful that Democrats began trying to copy it, so that since 1980 the entire US political system has lurched toward ever-increasing economic inequality, globalization, imperialism, and militarism.

So what did the Boomers do after 1980?

Having already taken a detour into the bleary world of recreational drugs, many of the more spirited Boomers now turned to gurus, meditation, and cults: politics was a bummer; if we really wanted to change the world we should change our heads first.

Other Boomers steered toward the stock market and scrambled up the corporate ladder. They got jobs, made money, and discovered that "greed is good." By the end of the decade it was apparent

that the Boomers were divided, with some upholding the Earth
Day vision, others honing their skills as right-wing radio talk show
hosts, and the rest just trying to get by.

Another Fork in the Road

Bill Clinton, the first Boomer president (born in 1946), elicited high
hopes among his generational peers feeling battered by a dozen
years of Reagan/Bush. But as governor of Arkansas, Clinton had already learned the necessity of obeying entrenched power-holders in
order to get along in politics. Moreover, by now the American gov-
ernmental-corporate system was far too large and complex, and had
far too much momentum behind it, to permit a fundamental change
in direction.

In the late 1960s and early '70s, many of us had believed that
when our generation eventually took over the reins of power we
would change the world. Well, here we were with one of our cohort
as president and the country was more deeply mired than ever in
the banality of consumerism. The WWII generation was increasingly filling obituary pages and populating nursing homes; now we
had no one to blame but ourselves. The generation of peace and
love had become the generation of SUVs and fast food.

It was clear that we had deluded ourselves by thinking of our cohort as united in its values, or by imagining that those values were
somehow immutable. Just as Brokaw's "greatest generation" had
started out in the 1930s battling the evils of unrestrained capitalism
and went on in the 1940s to fight the menace of fascism only to end
by electing Nixon, Reagan, and Bush and supporting the Vietnam
war, we were now doing something similar.

This is not to say that all of our number had sold out: we could
count as generational heroes and heroines thousands of scientists,
activists, artists, musicians, and writers who kept alive the Earth Day
ideal of a society that lives in harmony with nature rather than para-
sitically destroying it. However, with each passing year that ideal
seemed ever more elusive — especially so following the 2000 election.

We watched as that election was stolen, and our outrage only grew as we saw prominent Democrats quietly acquiescing to the evisceration of much of what was left of American democracy. The events of 9/11 jolted even the drowsiest awake, and some of us began paying attention as never before when we realized that mainstream news organizations were failing to ask the most obvious questions about the events — about the mysterious collapse of the towers, the failure of officials to dispatch jet fighters, the immediate confiscation and destruction of evidence, the suspicious airline stock trades, the thwarted warnings, and much more. With the invasions of Afghanistan and Iraq, the detentions in Guantanamo, and the passage of the USA Patriot Act, it became clear that the US had entered an entirely new historical period. The current president-by-decree was another Boomer, but his shortcomings didn't end with rampant corruption among his appointees and the simple-mindedness he so obviously exhibited: he was, in the words of George Washington University psychiatrist Dr. Justin Frank, "an untreated alcoholic with paranoid and megalomaniac tendencies," and his cronies were evidently dedicated neo-fascists with every intention of turning America into a Disneyland Reich. That they were in some ways ridiculously inept made them all the more dangerous.

In response, some Boomers honed their political consciousness. Political documentaries and blogs proliferated like wildflowers in springtime.

Elections came and went, and widespread disgust with the disastrous ongoing occupation of Iraq eventually handed Congress to the Democrats. But there was never broad public discussion of the real issue that will impact our lives in the next few years — the generation that grew up expecting always *more* will soon be faced with *less*. The nation, now hallucinating uncontrollably from toxic exposure to Fox News, is in debt to the point that no conceivable decision made today will prevent a devastating implosion of the US economy, especially in view of the impending oil and gas peaks.

It may seem cynical to some if I say that it is too late to salvage America's political system, its economy, its suburban way of life; that it is even too late to contemplate an easy and peaceful transition to a *different* socio-ecological reality. But as far as I can tell, these are the facts. That possibility probably died in 1980. As they say these days, *get over it.*

This doesn't mean that life will end tomorrow. The American dream is going down, yet we still have some control over *how* it goes down. And it is in this remaining arena of choice that the post-World War II cohort might partially redeem itself.

During the next two decades we Boomers will be our society's elders. We will have amassed considerable financial capital, as well as human capital in the forms of competence, credibility, and connections. How will we use this capital?

If we use it for any purpose other than to help awaken all and sundry to our collective plight, and to lead a change of course toward a peaceful, local, slow, and self-limiting post-fossil-fuel way of life, even if that goal may not be immediately attainable, it will all have been wasted.

In the decades ahead we will be going through hell. That is an awful thing to contemplate, but the only alternative to accepting the fact is to live in denial until the reality is inescapable and our room for maneuvering is even more restricted than it has already become. What we must do now is lay the groundwork for collective survival. We must build lifeboats, or support the younger lifeboat-builders among us. If we do this, there will be local centers of self-reliance around which a new culture of true sustainability can begin to coalesce. Maybe people who are around decades from now will then be able to contemplate the creation of ecotopia — let us hope so.

This is not the grandiose project we imagined for ourselves back in the 1960s and '70s. We thought that we ourselves would usher in the New Age, but that possibility is extinguished. We Boomers have stolen much from the future generations; the main question remaining is, can we now give them back at least the possibility that they might build the world we once dreamed of?

10

A Letter From the Future

GREETINGS TO YOU, people of the year 2007! You are living in the year of my birth; I am one hundred years old now, writing to you from the year 2107. I am using the last remnants of the advanced physics that scientists developed during your era, in order to send this electronic message back in time to one of your computer networks. I hope that you receive it, and that it will give you reason to pause and reflect on your world and what actions to take with regard to it.

Of myself I shall say only what it is necessary to say: I am a survivor. I have been extremely fortunate on many occasions and in many ways, and I regard it as something of a miracle that I am here to compose this message. I have spent much of my life attempting to pursue the career of historian, but circumstances have compelled me also to learn and practice the skills of farmer, forager, guerrilla fighter, engineer — and now physicist. My life has been long and eventful . . . but that is not what I have gone to so much trouble to convey to you. It is what I have witnessed during this past century that I feel compelled to tell you by these extraordinary means.

You are living at the end of an era. Perhaps you cannot understand that. I hope that by the time you have finished reading this letter, you will.

I want to tell you what is important for you to know, but you may find some of this information hard to absorb. Please have patience with me. I am an old man and I don't have time for niceties. The communication device I am using is quite unstable and there's no telling how much of my story will actually get through to you. Please pass it along to others. It will probably be the only such message you will ever receive.

Since I don't know how much information I will actually be able to convey, I'll start with the most important items, ones that will be of greatest help in your understanding of where your world is headed.

Energy has been the central organizing — or should I say, *dis*organizing? — principle of this century. Actually, in historical retrospect, I would have to say that energy was the central organizing principle of the nineteenth and twentieth centuries as well. People discovered new energy sources — coal, then petroleum — in the nineteenth century, and then invented all sorts of new technologies to make use of this freshly released energy. Transportation, manufacturing, agriculture, lighting, heating, communication — all were revolutionized, and the results reached deep into the lives of everyone in the industrialized world. Everybody became utterly dependent on the new gadgets: on imported, chemically fertilized food; on chemically synthesized and fossil-fuel-delivered therapeutic drugs; on the very idea of perpetual growth (after all, it would always be possible to produce *more* energy to fuel *more* transportation and manufacturing — wouldn't it?).

Well, if the nineteenth and twentieth centuries were the upside of the growth curve, this past century has been the downside — the cliff. It should have been perfectly obvious to everyone that the energy sources on which they were coming to rely were exhaustible. Somehow the thought never sank in very deep. I suppose that's because people generally tend to get used to a certain way of life, and from then on they don't think about it very much. That's true today, too. The young people now have never known anything different; they take for granted our way of life — scavenging among the remains of industrial civilization for whatever can be put to immediate use — as though this is how people have always lived, as if this is how we were meant to live. That's why I've always been attracted to history, so that I could get some perspective on human societies as they change through time. But I'm digressing. Where was I?

Yes — the energy crisis. Well, it all started around the time I was born. Folks then thought it would be brief, that it was just a political or technical problem, that soon everything would get back to normal. They didn't stop to think that "normal," in the longer-term historical sense, meant living on the energy budget of incoming sunlight and the vegetative growth of the biosphere. Perversely, they thought "normal" meant using fossil energy like there was no tomorrow. And, I guess, there almost wasn't.

At first, most people thought the shortages could be solved with "technology." However, in retrospect that's quite ludicrous. After all, their modern gadgetry had been invented to *use* a temporary abundance of energy. It didn't *produce* energy. Yes, there were the nuclear reactors (heavens, those things turned out to be nightmares!), but of course nuclear power came from uranium, another non-renewable resource. Then there were photovoltaic panels, which were a much better idea—except for the fact that some of the crucial materials, like gallium and indium, were also rare, quickly depleting substances. Moreover, making the panels ate up a substantial amount of the power the panels themselves generated during their lifetime. Nevertheless, quite a few of them were built — I wish that more had been! — and many are still operating (that's what's powering the device that allows me to transmit this signal to you from the future).

Solar power was a good idea; its main drawback was simply that it was incapable of satisfying people's energy-guzzling habits. With the exhaustion of fossil fuels, *no* technology could have maintained the way of life that people had gotten used to. But it took quite a while for many to realize that. Their pathetic faith in technology turned out to be almost religious in character, as though their gadgets were votive objects connecting them with an invisible but omnipotent god capable of overturning the laws of thermodynamics.

Naturally, some of the first effects of the energy shortages showed up as economic recessions, followed by an endless depression. The economists had been operating on the basis of their own religion — an absolute, unshakable faith in the Market-as-God and in supply-and-demand. They figured that if oil started to run out, the price would rise, offering incentives for research into alternatives. But the economists never bothered to think this through. If they had, they would have realized that the revamping of society's entire energy infrastructure would take decades, while the price signal from resource shortages would come at the exact moment some hypothetical replacement would be needed. Moreover, they should have realized that there *was no substitute* capable of fully replacing the energy resources they had come to rely on.

The economists could think only in terms of money; basic necessities like water and energy only showed up in their calculations in terms of dollar cost, which made them functionally interchangeable with everything else that could be priced — oranges, airliners, diamonds, baseball cards, whatever. But, in the last analysis, basic resources weren't interchangeable with other economic goods at all: you couldn't drink baseball cards, no matter how big or valuable your collection, once the water ran out. Nor could you eat dollars, if nobody had food to sell. And so, after a certain point, people started to lose faith in their money. And as they did so, they realized that *faith* had been the only thing that made money worth anything in the first place. Currencies just collapsed, first in one country, then in another. There was inflation, deflation, barter, and thievery of every imaginable kind as matters sorted themselves out.

In the era when I was born, commentators used to liken the global economy to a casino. A few folks were making trillions of dollars, euros, and yen trading in currencies, companies, and commodity futures. None of these people were actually doing anything useful; they were just laying down their bets and, in many cases, raking in colossal winnings. If you followed the economic chain, you'd see that all of that money was coming out of ordinary people's pockets ... but that's another story. Anyway: all of that economic activity depended on energy, on global transportation and communication, and on faith in the currencies. Early in the 21st century, the global casino went bust. Gradually, a new metaphor became operational. We went from global casino to village flea market.

With less energy available each year, and with unstable currencies plaguing transactions, manufacturing and transportation shrank in scale. It didn't matter how little Nike paid its workers in Indonesia: once shipping became prohibitively expensive, profits from the globalization of its operations vanished. But Nike couldn't just start up factories back in the States again; all of those factories had been closed decades earlier. The same with all the other clothing manufacturers, electronics manufacturers, and so on. All of that local manufacturing infrastructure had been destroyed to make way for globalization, for cheaper goods, for bigger corporate profits. And now, to recreate that infrastructure would require a huge financial and energy investment — just when money and energy were in ever-shorter supply.

Stores were empty. People were out of work. How were they to survive? The only way was by endlessly recycling all the used stuff that had been manufactured before the energy crisis. At first, after the initial economic shock waves, people were selling their stuff on Internet auctions — while there was still electricity. When it became clear that lack of reliable transportation made delivery of the goods problematic, people started selling stuff on street corners so they could pay their rents and mortgages and buy food. But after the currency collapse, that didn't make sense either, so people began just trading stuff, refurbishing it, using it however they could in order to get by. The cruel irony was that most of their stuff consisted of cars and electronic gadgets that nobody could afford to operate anymore. Worthless! Anybody who had human-powered hand tools and knew how to use them was wealthy indeed — and still is.

Industrial civilization sure produced a hell of a lot of junk during its brief existence. Over the past 50 or 60 years, folks have dug up just about every landfill there ever was, looking for anything that could be useful. What a god-awful mess! With all due respect, I have always had a hard time understanding why — and even *how* — you people could take billions of tons of invaluable, ancient, basic resources and turn them into mountains of stinking garbage, with almost no measurable period of practical use in between! Couldn't you at least have made *durable, well-designed* stuff? I must say that the quality of the tools, furniture, houses, and so on that we have inherited from you — and are forced to use, given that few of us are capable of replacing them — is pretty dismal.

Well, I apologize for those last remarks. I don't mean to be nasty or rude. Actually some of the hand tools left behind are quite good. But you have to understand: the industrial way of life to which you have become accustomed will have horrific consequences for your children and grandchildren.

I can vaguely remember seeing — when I was very young, maybe five or six — some old television shows from the 1950s: *Ozzie and Harriet...Father Knows Best...Lassie.* They portrayed an innocent world, one in which children grew up in small communities surrounded by friends and family. All problems were easily dealt with by adults who were mostly kind and wise. It all seemed so stable and benign.

When I was born, that world, if it had ever really existed, was long gone. By the time I was old enough to know much about what was happening on the bigger scene, society was beginning to come apart at the seams. It started with electricity blackouts — just a few hours at a time at first. At the same time the natural gas shortages clicked in. Not only were we cold most of the winter, but the blackouts got dramatically worse because so much electricity was being produced using natural gas. Meanwhile the oil and gasoline shortages were worsening. At this point — I guess I was a young teenager then — the economy was in tatters and there was political chaos.

By the time I was an older teenager, a certain identifiable attitude was developing among the young people. It was a feeling of utter contempt for anyone over a certain age — maybe 30 or 40. The adults had consumed so many resources, and now there were none left for their own children. Of course, when those adults were younger they had just been doing what everybody else was doing. They figured it was normal to cut down ancient forests for wood pulp for their phone books, pump every last gallon of oil to power their SUVs, or flick on the air conditioner if they were a little too warm. For the kids of my generation, all of that was just a dim memory. What we knew was very different. We were living in darkness, with shortages of food and water, with riots in the streets, with people begging on street corners, with unpredictable weather, with pollution and garbage that could no longer be carted away and hidden from sight. For us, the adults were the enemy.

In some places, the age wars remained just a matter of simmering resentment. In others, there were random attacks on older people. In still others, there were systematic purges. I'm ashamed to say that, while I didn't actually physically attack any older people, I did participate in the shaming and name-calling. Those poor old folks — some of them still quite young, from my present perspective! — were just as confused and betrayed as we kids were. I can imagine myself in their shoes. Try to do the same: try to remember the last time you went to a store to buy something and the store didn't have it. (This little thought exercise is a real stretch for me, since I haven't been in a "store" that actually had much of anything for several decades, but I'm trying to put this in terms that you will understand.) Did you feel frustrated? Did you get angry, thinking, "I drove all the way here for this thing, and now I'm going to have to drive all the way across town to another store to get it"? Well, multiply that frustration and anger by a thousand, ten thousand. This is what people were going through every day, with regard to just about every consumer item, service, or bureaucratic necessity they had grown accustomed to. Moreover, those adults had lost most of what they had in the economic crash. And now gangs of kids were stealing whatever was left and heaping scorn on them as they did so. That must have been devastating for them. Unbearable.

Now that I'm so ancient myself, I have a little more tolerance for people. We're all just trying to get by, doing the best we can.

I suppose you're curious to know more about what has happened during this past century — the politics, wars, revolutions. Well, I'll tell you what I know, but there's a lot that I don't. For the last 60 years or so we haven't had anything like the global communications networks that used to exist. There are large parts of the world about which I know almost nothing.

As you can imagine, when the energy resource shortages hit the

United States and the economy started to go into a tailspin (it's interesting that I still use that word: only the oldest among us, such as myself, have ever seen an airplane tailspin, nose-dive, or even fly), people became angry and started looking around for someone to blame. Of course, the government didn't want to be the culprit, so those bastards in power (sorry, I still don't have much sympathy for them) did what political leaders have always done — they created a foreign enemy. They sent warships, bombers, missiles, and tanks off across the oceans for heaven-knows-what grisly purpose. People were told that this was being done to protect their "American Way of Life." Well, there was nothing on Earth that could have accomplished that. It was the American Way of Life that was the problem!

The generals managed to kill a few million people. Actually, it could have been tens or hundreds of millions, even billions for all I know; the news media were never very clear on that, since they were censored by the military. There were antiwar protests in the streets, and some of the protestors were rounded up and put in concentration camps. The government became utterly fascistic in its methods toward the end. There were local uprisings and brutal crackdowns. But it was all for nothing. The wars only depleted what few resources were still available, and after a few horrible years the central government just collapsed. Ran out of gas.

Speaking of political events, it's worth noting that in the early years of the shortages, the existing political philosophies had very little to offer that was helpful. The right-wingers were completely devoted to shielding the wealthy from blame and shifting all of the pain onto poor people and overseas scapegoats. Meanwhile, the Left was so habituated to fighting corporate meanies that it couldn't grasp the fact that the problems now facing society couldn't be solved by economic redistribution. Personally, as a historian, I tend to be much more sympathetic to the Left because I think that the amount of wealth a few people accumulated was just obscene. I suspect that a hell of a lot of suffering could have been averted if all of that wealth had been spread around early on, when the money was worth something. But to hear some of the leftist leaders talk, you'd think that once all the corporations had been reined in, once the billionaire plutocrats had been relieved of their riches, everything would be fine. Well, everything wasn't going to be fine, no way.

So here were these two political factions fighting to the death, blaming each other, while everybody around them was starving or going crazy. What the people really needed was just some basic commonsense information and advice, somebody to tell them the truth — their way of life was coming to an end — and to offer them some sensible collective survival strategies.

Much of what has happened during the past century was what you have every reason to expect on the basis of your scientists' forecasts: we have seen dramatic climate shifts, species extinctions, and horrible epidemics, just as the ecologists at the turn of the 21st century warned there would be. I don't think that's a matter of much satisfaction to those ecologists' descendants. Getting to say "I told you so" is paltry comfort in this situation. Tigers and whales are gone, and probably tens of thousands of other species; but our lack of reliable global communications makes it difficult for anyone to know just which species and where. The last I heard, the oceans have been mostly empty of life for decades. For me, songbirds are a fond but distant memory. I suppose my counterparts in China or Africa have their own long lists.

Climate Change has been a real problem for growing food. You never know from one year to the next what swarms of unfamiliar insects will show up. For a year or two or three, all we get is rain. Then there's drought for the next five or six. It's much worse than a nuisance; it's life-threatening. That's just one of the factors that has led to the dramatic reduction in human population during the last century.

Many people call it "The Die-off." Others call it "The Pruning," "The Purification," or "The Cleansing." Some terms are more palatable than others, but there really are no nice ways to describe the actual events — wars, epidemics, famines.

Food and water have been big factors in all of this. Fresh, clean water has been scarce for decades now. One way to make young people mad at me is to tell them stories about how folks in the old days used to pour millions upon millions of gallons of water on their lawns. When I describe to them how flush toilets worked, they just can't bear it. Some of them think I'm making this stuff up! These days water is serious business. If you waste it, somebody's likely to die.

Starting many decades ago, people began — by necessity — to learn how to grow their own food. Not everyone was successful, and there was a lot of hunger. One of the frustrating things was the lack of good seeds. Very few people knew anything about saving seeds from one season to the next, so existing seed stocks were depleted very quickly. There was also a big problem with all the modern hybrid varieties: few of the garden vegetables that were planted would produce good seeds for the next year. The genetically engineered plants were even worse, causing all sorts of ecological problems that we're still dealing with, particularly the killing off of bees and other beneficial insects. The "suicide seeds" developed by the designer-gene seed companies to protect patent rights were absolutely the worst: while those strains disappeared very quickly once the distribution system started to come apart, the millions of people dependent on them for food had nothing else to plant — or eat. That story is part of our collective mythology now, and is just one of the reasons that the seeds of good open-pollinated food plants are like gold to us.

I did some traveling by foot and on horseback when I was younger, in my fifties and sixties, and we continue to get some sporadic reports from the outside world. From what I've seen and heard, it seems that people in different places have coped in different ways and with widely varying degrees of success. Ironically, perhaps, the indigenous people who were most persecuted by civilization are probably doing the best. They still retained a lot of knowledge of how to live simply on the land. In some places, people are dwelling together in makeshift rural communes; other folks are trying to survive in what's left of the great urban centers, ripping up concrete and growing what they can as they recycle and trade all the old junk that was left behind when people fled the cities in the 1920s.

Speaking as a historian, one of my biggest frustrations is the rapid disappearance of knowledge. You people had a mania for putting most of your important information on electronic storage media and acid-laden paper — which are disintegrating very quickly. For the most part, all we have are fading photographs, random books, and crumbling magazines.

A few of our young people look at the old magazine ads and wonder what it must have been like to live in a world with jet airplanes, electricity, and sports cars. It must have been utopia, paradise! Others among us are not so sanguine about the past. I suppose that's part of my job as a historian: to remind everyone that the advertising images were only one side of a story; it was the other side of that story — the rampant exploitation of nature and people, the blindness to consequences — that led to the horrors of the past century.

You're probably wondering if I have any good news, anything encouraging to say about the future of your world. Well, as with most things, it depends on your perspective. Many of the survivors learned valuable lessons. They learned what's important in life and what isn't. They learned to treasure good soil, viable seeds, clean water, unpolluted air, and friends you can count on. They learned how to take charge of their own lives, rather than expecting to be taken care of by some government or corporation. There are no "jobs" now, so people's time is all their own. They think for themselves more. Partly as a result of that, the old religions have largely fallen by the wayside, and folks have rediscovered spirituality in nature and in their local communities. The kids today are eager to learn and to create their own culture. The traumas of industrial civilization's collapse are mostly in the past; that's history now. It's a new day.

Can you change my past, which is your future? I don't know. There are all sorts of logical contradictions inherent in that question. I can barely understand the principles of physics that allow me to transmit this signal to you. Possibly, as a result of reading this letter, you might do something that would change my world. Maybe you could save a forest or a species, or preserve some heirloom seeds, or help prepare yourselves and the rest of the population for the coming energy shortages. Maybe you could talk a lot of people into leaving fossil fuels in the ground, where they belong. My life might be altered as a result. Then, I suppose this letter would change, as would your experience of reading it. And as a result of that, you'd take *different* actions. We would have set up some kind of cosmic feedback loop between past and future. It's pretty interesting to think about.

Speaking of physics, maybe I should mention that I've come to accept a view of history based on what I've read about chaos theory. According to the theory, in chaotic systems small changes in initial conditions can lead to big changes in outcomes. Well, human society and history are chaotic systems. Even though most of what people do is determined by material circumstances, they still have some wiggle room, and what they do with that can make a significant difference down the line. In retrospect, it appears that human survival in the 21st century hinged on many small and seemingly insignificant efforts by marginalized individuals and groups in the 20th century. The anti-nuclear movement, the conservation movement, the anti-biotech movement, the organic food and gardening movements, indigenous peoples' resistance movements, the tiny organizations devoted to seed saving — all had a profound and positive impact on later events.

I suppose that, logically speaking, if you were to alter the web of causation leading up to my present existence, it is possible that events might transpire that would preclude my being here. In that case, this letter would constitute history's most bizarre suicide note! But that is a risk I am willing to take. Do what you can. Change history! And while you're at it, be kind to one another. Don't take anything or anyone for granted.

11

Talking Ourselves to Extinction

LANGUAGE IS A POWERFUL meta-tool that dramatically amplifies cooperative human efforts to control the environment. Language also opens the possibility for religion and science — which otherwise would not exist. Language helped generate our current ecological dilemma. Can language help solve it?

In systems theory and evolutionary biology, the word *emergence* describes the development of complex systems or organs; an *emergent* phenomenon is one based on the interaction of simpler elements but whose characteristics cannot be predicted based on a thorough knowledge of those elements. In the course of a species' evolution a variation may appear that is retained because it confers an advantage in terms of existing functions; but once in place, the new characteristic may act in combination with other capacities of the organism to make truly novel and unexpected functions possible. Organs for sight and hearing probably originated as emergent phenomena. Life itself has been described as an emergent property of matter, and sensation and mind are emergent properties of higher organisms.

Human societies are dynamic, complex systems, and most of their signal features are understandable as emergent phenomena. It is a fascinating thought exercise (I've been at it for two decades now) to attempt to trace events in the past in order to identify the most decisive developments that enabled the emergence of industrial civilization. Of course, societal complexity (defined by the variety of tools, artifacts, and social roles) depends on humans' ability to capture increasing amounts of energy from their environment, and so the genetic and social attributes that facilitate energy capture are crucial. Which of those attributes are keys to understanding the entire process?

Clearly, most of the emergent features of complex societies (their economies, technologies, and governments) depend on language. Now, language itself is an emergent phenomenon, a link in a long chain of them; however, it was a profoundly consequential one. In the grand edifice of human society, language should be considered a foundation stone.

The questions of how and when language evolved are hotly debated. Some archaeologists argue that the relatively sudden appearance, roughly 40,000 years ago, of counting sticks and new kinds of hunting tools suggests that language arose then. However, humans — including Neanderthals — were anatomically capable of speech much earlier; indeed, there is fossil evidence that the main areas of the brain associated with language (Broca's area and Wernicke's area) started to enlarge up to 1.5 million years ago. Moreover, humans' ability to spread to regions outside of Africa, and especially to islands, may have depended upon their use of language to convey information and intention and to coordinate tasks. It may be that we have been using language so long that our brains, throats, and chests have all evolved in tandem. The situation is likely similar to what has happened in the computer industry over the past few decades: just as hardware and software developers work cooperatively, one designing according to the needs and capacities of the other, our own internal hardware (brain and speech faculties) and software (language) have become, in a sense, made for one another.

Part of the problem in determining when and how language arose may lie in definitions. The term *language* can refer in a vague or general sense to any sort of communication; but this usage is not always helpful. All animals communicate using sound, color, scent, or gesture. Even plants and fungi communicate with one another using chemicals and gene packets transmitted via soil or air. Human language differs from these kinds of information transfer in its level of abstraction, its multiplicity of symbols, and the complexity of its grammar (or system of rules for the manipulation of symbols). It is one thing to signal a somatic or emotional state or a general intention, but quite another to discuss events, including hypothetical ones, in the future or the past, or in distant places.

Language made these things possible, but much more as well. Language generated our peculiarly human form of self-awareness: we can talk about ourselves, talk about talking, and think about thinking. Our relationship with our environment also changed, as language enabled us to coordinate our thinking and behavior across time and distance in a way that was unprecedented, making us a far more formidable species (compare the population size and environmental impacts of humans today with those of chimpanzees or gorillas). Writing only exacerbated these trends, heightening the level of abstraction in language and widening our ability to convey thoughts and align collective action. If talking helped organize effective hunting bands, writing enabled the formation of nation states. Add the printing press, radio, television, and fossil fuels, and here we are today.

But with language came an array of unintended consequences — which, of course, is just another name for emergent phenomena.

Language and Religion

"In the beginning was the Word," proclaims the Gospel according to John. In Genesis, creation commences with a series of spoken commands, starting with "Let there be light." The creation stories of the ancient Egyptians, Celts, and Mayans likewise emphasized the generative potency of language.

This striking coincidence, noted by many scholars of world mythology, cloaks a supreme irony: while religion ascribes magical power to words, there are reasons to think that religion itself may be an inevitable though accidental outgrowth of language.

It is interesting to speculate whether non-human animals have awareness of something that humans might recognize as a spiritual dimension of existence. Do dogs and cats have near-death or out-of-body experiences? Do birds experience awe and wonder when watching the sunrise? There is no way to know for sure. In any case, it is fairly clear that no non-human species has developed a religion — if we mean by this term an organized set of beliefs about the supernatural, and a set of practices oriented to the service or worship of a divine being or beings.

Why not? What is unique about humans that would lead us to construct religions? Are we set apart because we alone possess souls? Or do our brains contain some unusual structure shared by no other animal? Research into neurotheology, while controversial, offers some clues: religious or spiritual experiences seem primarily to be associated with the right temporal lobe of the neocortex, implying that feelings associated with such experiences are normal features of brain function under extreme circumstances. Nevertheless, it is likely that the problem of religion is as much an issue of "software" (language) as it is one of "hardware" (brain structure).

Let us suppose that language was initially used only for practical purposes such as coordinating hunting efforts. Slowly, haphazardly, people must have developed rudimentary elements of vocabulary and grammar, often in order to aid with planning — an activity inherently implying the senses of location, time, cause, effect, and intention. Women, men, and children began to make simple sentences to ask and explain — *who, what, where, when,* and *why?* Once the ability to pose and answer such questions was in place, it inevitably began to be applied to less immediately pressing concerns. The Pleistocene hunter went from asking, "Where did these bison come from?" to "Where did stars, the Moon, the Sun, and people come from?" Hence the mythologies of aboriginal peoples everywhere are rich in origin stories. Language was seductive in its power: once a tiny morsel of reality had been verbally nibbled off, its incomplete digestion provoked a recurring hunger to take another and yet another bite, and eventually to swallow the world whole.

As power over the environment grew, as society became more complex and formidable, religion mutated accordingly. Hunter-gatherers saw nature as alive and filled with spiritual presences that could directly be engaged by way of shamanic practices. Such beliefs and behaviors grew out of these people's direct interaction with their environment, and fit their needs for social cohesion within an egalitarian context. With division of labor and thus a hierarchical organization of society came full-time specialists who got their food not directly from nature but from other humans; some of these specialists were spiritual intermediaries (priests) who appealed to sky gods detached from nature and the lives of commoners. With writing, myths about the gods could be codified and carried to distant lands (this story is told in fascinating detail in Bruce Lerro's *From Earth Spirits to Sky Gods*).

German orientalist Max Müller (1823–1900), who virtually created the discipline of comparative religion, put the matter succinctly by asserting that mythology is a "disease of language."

Perhaps the word *disease* seems too harsh. After all, mythology has its uses as well: as Joseph Campbell never tired of saying, myth gives us meaning. And surely meaning is a good thing. Nevertheless, the human need for meaning again highlights our obsessive and dependent relationship with language. Meaning is always attached to symbols: we invest a symbol with meaning, and that meaning is conveyed to whoever correctly interprets the symbol. We see a sentence written in an unfamiliar language and we wonder, "What does it mean?" As we have become ever more hooked on linguistic symbols, we have come to see nearly everything as if it were a sign for something else. We look to stars, tea leaves, and coincidences for meaning. The universe is talking to us! Myths are verbal narratives that seek to unpack the meaning of existence. We seldom wonder why it is that life must have meaning in order to be satisfying. Is it possible that existence could be sufficient unto itself, with no need for an embedded message?

Religion consists of more than just mythology, though. Surely religion evolved at least partly to coordinate and moderate collective behavior via systems of morality and ethics which, in their most basic forms, appear to be genetically coded. The senses of good and evil, of honor and shame, have become such powerful internal motivators for humans that even most atheists are continually compelled by them. There is nothing quite like this among other species, whose behavior tends to be less learned and more genetically coded, and who therefore do not engage in the practices of rewarding or punishing one another's behavior nearly to the same degree we do. Ironically, morality often contributes to humans' most brutal acts, which have little precedent in other animals (witch burnings, as just one example, were morally motivated).

Nevertheless, the development of complex societies would surely have been difficult if not impossible without morality — which had previously often been turned toward ecological ends, as early societies codified their needs to moderate reproduction, avoid incest, and protect natural resources via their taboos ("Do not kill the red kangaroo during its mating season!"). But then, once religion and society had mutually mutated in the direction of abstraction and complexity, morality became at least partly unhinged from environmental and genetic necessity and began increasingly to adhere to written myths about the verbally hallucinated sky gods.

From an ecological point of view, the results were sometimes inadvertently salutary: religious wars (such as the Crusades) helped temporarily to moderate human population levels — though comparable results had been achieved by hunter-gatherer societies using gentler methods such as herbal contraception. Some religions also promoted celibacy among priests, monks, and nuns, again helping to stem population growth. But as people's verbal obsessions began to be taken up with myths that had more to do with consolidating the power of religious elites than with regulating people's relations with the natural world, religion served increasingly as an instrument of social and ecological conquest.

Nevertheless, if language muddied humans' connections with nature by way of verbal speculation, regimentation, and hallucination, it also fostered a countervailing tendency.

Grammar, Reason, Logic, and Evidence

Other animals observe, plan, draw conclusions from experience, and continually revise their mental pictures of reality. These capacities, the foundations of *reason*, are not uniquely human. *Logic*, which is the study of reasoning, is uniquely human, however, because it requires language.

Logic is inherent in grammar, which people developed and used long before there were grammar schools, or schools of any sort, and young children still absorb the basic rules of grammar intuitively without having to be drilled in them. In language, each coherent packet of meaning (such as a sentence) must adhere to some agreed-upon standards if it is to be useful. In this regard a sentence is like a mathematical equation (mathematics, after all, is itself a language): before an equation can be correct or incorrect, it must conform to basic rules. Unlike the statements "2+6=8" and "3+4=9" (one of which we would recognize as being true, the other false), the statement "=5+7 –" cannot be said to be true or false; it is simply unintelligible because it is not organized as a complete equation according to the rules of arithmetic. (Quantum physicist Wolfgang Pauli, who was known for his abhorrence of sloppy thinking, once famously commented that another scientist's work was "not even wrong.")

Grammar and logic give us the basis for making comprehensible statements about the world; linking logic with empirical evidence helps us formulate true statements and recognize when statements are false. This, again, is a long-standing practice: millennia before the scientific method was codified, people relied on feedback between language and sensory data to develop an accurate understanding of the world. Are the salmon running yet? Let's go look.

However, not all possible statements could be checked empirically. If someone said, "These berries taste good," that was at least a matter for investigation, even if everyone didn't agree. But the situation was more complicated if someone said, "The volcano smokes — that must be because the gods are angry; and if the gods are angry it must be because we haven't provided enough sacrifices." Unlike the observation that the volcano was smoking, the following two statements and the reasoning behind them had no verifiable basis — unless the gods could be called into the village commons and publicly queried about their moods and motives (the attempt to do so may have led to the origin of shamanic trance mediumship). This was magical thinking — reasoning based on mere correlation rather than an empirically, publicly verifiable chain of causation.

It was inevitable that magical thinking would flourish given that there were so many subjects of interest for which empirical investigation was impractical or impossible. That situation continues: there is still no empirical basis for answering, once and for all and to everyone's satisfaction, questions like, "Does God exist?", "Who am I?", "What happens to us when we die?", or "What is the greatest good?"

Yet however strong the temptation to engage in it, magical thinking when tied to religion failed to provide much practical help in industry or commerce. As these limits came to be appreciated, and as industry and commerce expanded, philosophers and students of nature began to construct the formalized system of inquiry known as the scientific method. Here was a way to obtain verifiable knowledge of the physical world; better still, it was knowledge that could often be used to practical effect. The method came to hand at a propitious time: wealth was flowing to Europe from the rest of the world due to colonization and slavery; meanwhile the development of metallurgy and simple heat engines had proceeded to the point where the energy of fossil fuels could be put to widespread use. When coupled with the project of technological invention, science and mathematics yielded undreamt-of power over the environment. When further coupled with capitalism (corporations, banking, and investment) and fossil fuels, the result was the industrial growth machine.

All of this would have been fine if we lived in an infinite sea of resources, but instead we inhabit a bounded, finite planet. Humanity had set a course toward disaster.

Language and the Ecological Dilemma

The ecological dilemma (which consists of the mutually rebounding impacts of population pressure, resource depletion, and habitat destruction) is certainly not unique to the modern industrial era; indeed, it is not unique even to humans. However, modern humans have created a dilemma for themselves of unprecedented scope and scale.

The dilemma, whether encountered by people or pigeons, is often a matter of the failure of success: the genetically engrained aims of the organism are to reproduce and to increase its energy capture, but its environment always has limited resources. Thus temporary population blooms (which are, in their way, evidence of biological success) are usually followed by a crash and die-off. In humans, the powers conferred by language, tools, and social organization have enabled many boom-and-bust cycles over the millennia. But the recent fossil fuel era has seen so much growth of population and consumption that there is an overwhelming likelihood of a crash of titanic proportions.

This should be glaringly obvious to everyone. Our ecologists have studied population blooms and crashes in other species. Our soil scientists appreciate the limits of modern agriculture. Our geologists understand perfectly well that fossil fuels are finite in quantity. And our mathematicians can easily calculate exponential growth rates to show how quickly population increase and resource depletion will outstrip our ability to satisfy even the most basic human needs. Verbal and mathematical logic, joined with empirical evidence, make an airtight case: we're headed toward a cliff.

But language also keeps most of us in the dark. This is partly because magical thinking is alive and well — and not just in churches and New Age seminars.

In the last couple of centuries, the magical thinking associated with religion, under assault from science, has found a new home in political and economic ideologies. Economics, which masquerades as a science, began as a branch of moral philosophy — which it still is in fact. For free-market ideologues, the market is God and profit is the ultimate good. We have used language to talk ourselves into the myth of progress — the belief that growth is always beneficial, and that there are no practical limits to the size of the human population or to the extent of renewable or even non-renewable natural resources we can use. This particular myth was an easy sell: it is an inherently welcome message (a version of "you can eat your cake and have it too") and it seemed to be confirmed by experience during a multi-generational period of unprecedented expansion based on the one-time-only consumption of Earth's hydrocarbon stores.

Meanwhile, at the business end of economic theory, masters of advertising, marketing, and public relations have learned deftly to manipulate symbols and images for emotional effect, sculpting the public's aspirations for comfort and prestige. This new kind of magical thinking *did* contribute to commerce and industry — and spectacularly so! (For historical details on this, see the BBC television documentary series "Century of Self" by Adam Curtis, and the books of Stuart Ewen.)

In politics, the 20th century saw battles between the quasi-religious ideologies of the left and right — Leninism, Stalinism, Fascism, Nazism, and Maoism, along with British "it's-for-your-own-good" colonialism and equally benevolent Yankee imperialism. In recent years, the political philosophy of Leo Strauss and his followers has come to the fore via the neoconservative members of the current Bush administration. Strauss taught a doctrine that is really just the explicit utterance of an implicit belief common among ruling elites — it is the duty of wise leaders to cloak their policies in potent patriotic and religious symbols and myths in order to galvanize the internal ethical imperatives of the masses. In other words, lies (if told by the right people for the right reasons) are not only good and necessary; they are the very foundation of responsible statecraft. On this basis, however, language ceases to provide a toolset for accurately mapping the world and instead becomes a mental haze enveloping society, preventing us collectively from grasping our situation. Only the rulers are expected (or allowed) to know the true score; but all too often they come to believe their own myths.

And so we live today in a fog of words so thick that it largely prevents us from seeing where we are or where we're headed. Language helps us understand, and at the same time prevents understanding. It enables reason and rationality, yet also frustrates them.

Simply put, language magnifies all of the conflicting priorities and potentials of the human organism.

Can Language Help Us Now?

It might seem that the solution to our quandary is a big dose of logic and empiricism. If only the matter were that simple.

Modern brain research explodes the notion that logic can exist in pristine isolation from emotional and somatic states: as neurologist Antonio Damasio explained in his book *Descartes' Error: Emotion, Reason, and the Human Brain,* emotion and reason are not separate; in fact, the latter is inherently dependent upon the former. Domasio explored the unusual case of Phineas Gage, a railroad construction foreman whose severe brain injury (a tamping iron was blown through his skull) prevented him from feeling emotions. While Gage remained intelligent and responsive after his accident, he lost the ability to make rational decisions and to reason, because his emotions were inaccessible to the process. Damasio argued that bodily senses give rise to emotions, which in turn provide the basis for rational (as well as irrational) thought. Thus our state of mind merely reflects our state of body, with emotion as the essential intermediary. The rational and emotional functions of language appear to be handled differently by the hemispheres of the brain: it seems that the left hemisphere processes verbiage that conveys linguistic meaning, while the right hemisphere processes verbal (as well as musical and other artistic) expression that conveys emotional content. There are indications that, in most people, the right hemisphere has a tendency to repress the free functioning of the left, thus making brain activity lopsided and dysfunctional while fomenting self-sabotaging internal conflict. This may be one reason we can appear perfectly rational in our pursuit of ends that are, from another perspective, just plain crazy.

Again, the organism wants energy, space, and the opportunity to reproduce itself. However, if every human's individual pursuit of those goals went unchecked, there could be no organized society because all collective effort would dissolve in continual one-on-one competition. Humans would go from bloom to crash with no period of stability between. As history has shown, an organized society can be quite effective at increasing human survival options and population levels.

Therefore the organism also needs to cooperate, to attenuate wants and desires, and to restrain reproduction. Accordingly we have developed innumerable customs, institutions, and moral strictures to promote moderation. The result is the battle of instinct against society that Freud agonized over (and largely mischaracterized) in *Civilization and Its Discontents*. In stable societies, a truce is struck that may last centuries or millennia. In our modern world, temporary success based on unique historical circumstances has led us to cast most self-limitation aside, and we have given ourselves perfectly good reasons for doing so. The truce is broken, and we are at war with nature and future generations.

Is it possible, now and quickly, to tame the organism's hunger for growth and head off catastrophe? Yes, in principle. One of the wonders of language is that it makes rapid societal change possible. Where another species would require centuries or millennia of genetic variation and natural selection to adapt itself to new conditions, we can shift our collective behavior in a matter of months or years, given language, media, and effective appeals to ethics. Whether it is possible to do so in the current situation, given the enormous growth momentum developed during the past two centuries, remains to be seen. Nevertheless, it is a useful exercise to imagine how a rapid surge toward collective self-limitation might come about.

An appeal would need to be made, on an ethical basis, to reduce consumption and alter personal aspirations. President Carter tried to do this when he suggested, in 1977, that solving the energy crisis was "the moral equivalent of war" — but sadly other politicians and the arbiters of economy and culture failed to back him up. To be successful, such an effort would require the enthusiastic participation of the advertising, public relations, and entertainment industries, as well as organized religions and all major political institutions. Leaders would have to engage the non-rational aspects of mass consciousness by playing upon our shared needs for meaning and myth, using verbal voodoo to alter attitudes and behavior as rapidly as possible. Wartime jingoism has accomplished something similar on many occasions in the past.

The campaign would have little chance of success if it were not also based on sound rational arguments, since purely emotional appeals would be rejected out of hand by the most intelligent and influential members of society. Moreover, if an attempt to change collective behavior were not based on empirically verifiable, survival-based necessity, it would amount to crass manipulation worthy of a Karl Rove or an Edward Bernays; hence its moral credibility would soon wane.

In the current instance, the rational basis for the appeal, and its centrality to our survival, are clear. Nothing is to be lost and every-thing to be gained by sharing accurate and relevant information about our situation; there is no need to exaggerate the threat.

Today precisely such an effort is already under way with regard to Climate Change. Al Gore and his famous movie have framed the crisis in moral terms, while hundreds of scientists, by endorsing the conclusions of the IPCC, have established a concurrent appeal to rationality.

As yet, the message does not have a sufficiently broad base of cultural support to curtail ongoing, richly-funded calls to buy, con-sume, and travel. Perhaps the addition of the Peak Oil message, by highlighting immediate economic and geopolitical threats posed by continued societal reliance on fossil fuels, will help broaden the coalition of support for needed change. But all of this will have to happen very quickly.

At this point, language is a given. For better or worse, we hu-mans are stuck with it, even if it arguably has contributed to crises that threaten us with extinction. One way or another, the way we deal with the enormous ecological challenge facing us will be medi-ated by words, words, and more words—some accurately reflecting the situation, others concealing it.

Meanwhile here we are, I writing, you reading. We share — I hope and assume — a commitment to logic and evidence, and to an ethic of collective human and non-human survival that transcends the myths of religion and progress.

There is no denying the satisfaction — even thrill — that comes when language hits its mark by dramatically aiding our understanding of what is by now an unimaginably complex human matrix. Perhaps the most we can do, now as before, though with more urgency than ever, is to harness that thrill by using language skillfully to describe and persuade; and meanwhile to act in ways that are congruent with the ethical content of our words.

Resources for Action

My hope in writing *Peak Everything* is not to leave readers in despair, but to impel them to action. There are many things we all can do to ease the transition from the century of growth to the century of contraction. The following are a two of the most important organizations helping to coordinate such efforts.

Over 150 Post Carbon groups have emerged in recent months, coordinated by the Post Carbon Institute (postcarbon.org). The **Relocalization Network** (relocalize.net) supports local Post Carbon groups as they work to develop and implement the strategy of relocalization in their communities. Relocalization Network Coordinators support the Network by providing on-line communication tools, developing resources, facilitating connections between local groups, and cultivating a sense of working together globally on local responses.

Those living in Britain may wish also to join the **Transition Towns Movement** (transitiontowns.org; www.transitionculture .org). The mission of this burgeoning movement is to inspire, inform, support and train communities as they consider, adopt and implement a coordinated transition away from fossil fuels and toward a renewable, local economy.

In addition, here are three websites offering news and discussion relevant to the subjects discussed in this book:

- Global Public Media (globalpublicmedia.com) provides audio, video, and print interviews and other materials
- Energy Bulletin (energybulletin.net) offers daily updated news on energy issues, highlighting subjects such as Peak Oil, renewable energy, climate change, and sustainability.
- The Oil Drum (theoildrum.com) features original analysis and discussion primarily relating to Peak Oil, but also touching on other fossil fuels, renewable energy, and transportation.

Notes

Introduction

1. From the *OPEC Bulletin*, November–December, 2006: "[A]ll in all, most would appear to agree that **peak oil output is not very far away for all of us. It could take place sometime within the next decade or so,** which in fact means that there is not much time left for a world economy to be driven largely by oil." Meanwhile, Claude Mandil, Executive Director of the International Energy Agency, speaking on the IEA *World Energy Outlook 2006,* had this to say: "WEO-2006 reveals that the energy future we are facing today, based on projections of current trends, is dirty, insecure and expensive." energybulletin.net/22042.html (Cited June 11, 2007)

2. Robert Hirsch et al. "Peaking of World Oil Production: Impacts, Mitigation and Risk Management," 2005. projectcensored.org/newsflash/the _hirsch_report.pdf (Cited June 11, 2007)

3. See also Kenneth S. Deffeyes, *Beyond Oil: The View from Hubbert's Peak.* Hill and Wang, 2005 and Roger D. Blanchard, *The Future of Global Oil Production: Facts, Figures, Trends and Projections, by Region.* McFarland, 2005.

4. Energy Watch Group. "Coal: Resources and Future Production." energy watchgroup.org/files/Coalreport.pdf (Cited June 11, 2007)

   See also Richard Heinberg. "Burning the Furniture." globalpublic media.com/richard_heinbergs_museletter_179_burning_the_furniture (Cited June 11, 2007)

5. Kevin McKern. "Trader Kev Explores the Commodity Peak Zeitgiest." kontentkonsult.com/blog/2006/01/peak_metals.html (Cited June 11, 2007). See also David Cohen, "Earth Audit," *New Scientist* May 23, 2007 issue 2605.

6. Energy Watch Group. "Uranium Resources and Nuclear Energy." December 2006. energiekrise.de/news/docs/specials2006/REO-Uran ium_5-12-2006.pdf (Cited June 11, 2007)

7. Ivan Illich. *Energy and Equity.* Calder & Boyars, 1974, p. 17.

8. World Income Inequality Database. wider.unu.edu/wiid/wiid.htm

9. James B. Davies, Susanna Sandstrom, Anthony Shorrocks, Edward N. Wolff. *The World Distribution of Household Wealth.* wider.unu.edu/resear ch/2006-2007/2006-2007-1/wider-wdhw-launch-5-12-2006/wider -wdhw-report-5-12-2006.pdf (Cited June 11, 2007)

10. We know this from the field research of anthropologists. See, for example, Marshall Sahlins, *Stone Age Economics*. Aldine, 1972.

11. Data for this paragraph are taken from Juliet B. Schor, *The Overworked American: The Unexpected Decline of Leisure*. Basic Books, 1993.

12. Phillip Johanson. "The Genuine Progress Indicator Shows Continued Decline in Quality of Life." socialfunds.com/news/article.cgi/117.html (Cited June 11, 2007)

13. Millenium Ecosystem Assessment. maweb.org/en/index.aspx (Cited June 11, 2007); Dan Moukerud. "Global warming is here, now what?" article.wn.com/view/2007/01/04/Global_warming_is_here_now_ what/ (Cited June 11, 2007)

14. Michael Klare. *Blood and Oil: The Dangers and Consequences of America's Growing Dependency on Imported Petroleum*. Metropolitan Books, 2004.

15. Thanks to my friend Chellis Glendinning, for her book *Waking Up in the Nuclear Age*, Beech Tree, 1987, which has been an inspiration in more ways than one.

16. Jason A. Merchey, ed. *Living a Life of Value*. Values of the Wise Press, 2006.

17. Richard Heinberg. *Fifty Million Farmers*. schumachersociety.org/publi cations/heinberg_06.html

Chapter 1

1. Lewis Mumford. "Authoritarian and Democratic Technics." Originally published in *Technology and Culture*, Vol. 5 No. 1, reprinted in John Zerzan and Carnes, eds. *Questioning Technology: Tool, Toy or Tyrant?* New Society, Publishers, 1991, p. 17.

2. John Zerzan. *Elements of Refusal*. Left Bank Books, 1988.

3. Lewis Mumford. *Technics and Human Development*. Harcourt, Brace, Jovanovich, 1966; *The Pentagon of Power*. Harcourt, Brace, Jovanovich, 1970, p. 146.

4. Richard Heinberg. *A New Covenant with Nature: Notes on the End of Civilization and the Renewal of Culture*. Quest Books, 1996.

5. Richard Heinberg. *The Party's Over: Oil, War and the Fate of Industrial Societies*. New Society Publishers, 2005, p. 26.

6. Marvin Harris. *Cultural Materialism: The Struggle for a Science of Culture*. Random House, 1979, pp. 56–58.

7. Zerzan's *Elements of Refusal* (Left Bank Books, 1988) includes chapters on time, language, number, art, agriculture, and domestication, arguing in each instance that the costs for each of these "advances" has far outweighed its benefit. Whether one agrees or disagrees with his opinion, he must be credited with consistency.

8. Robert Adler. "Entering a dark age of innovation." *NewScientist.com* news service, July 2, 2005. newscientist.com/article.ns?id=dn7616 (Cited June 12, 2007)

Chapter 2

1. Fernand Braudel, in his classic study *The Structures of Everyday Life: The Limits of the Possible* (translated from French by Sian Reynolds, University of California Press, 1992), notes that, "Famine recurred so insistently for centuries on end that it became incorporated into man's biological regime and built into his daily life.... France, by any standard a privileged country, is reckoned to have experienced 10 *general* famines during the tenth century; 26 in the eleventh; 2 in the twelfth; 4 in the fourteenth; 7 in the fifteenth; 13 in the sixteenth; 11 in the seventeenth and 16 in the eighteenth." (pp. 73–74).

2. Statistics gathered by Jennifer Bresee from USDA website: usda.gov (Cited December 11, 2006)

3. Pearce Hammond and Brian Gamble. "Alternative Fuels." *Simmons Energy Monthly,* Sept. 15, 2006, simmonsco-intl.com/files/091506%20Alternative.pdf (Cited June 12, 2007)

4. I recommend the DVD documentary, *The Power of Community: How Cuba Survived Peak Oil.* Community Solution, 2006. communitysolution.org/cuba.html (Cited June 12, 2007)

5. The story of the victory garden movements is recounted in David M. Tucker, *Kitchen Gardening in America: A History,* Iowa State University Press, 1993, in the chapter "Victory Gardening" pp. 121–139.

6. David Holmgren. *Permaculture: Principles and Pathways Beyond Sustainability.* Holmgren Design Services, 2002, p. 27.

7. Brainy Encyclopedia. brainyencyclopedia.com/b/bi/biointensive.html (Cited June 12, 2007)

8. "Indian Line Farm – Model for Farmland Preservation and Conservation." smallisbeautiful.org/clts/indian.html (Cited June 12, 2007)

9. Kirkpatrick Sale. *Human Scale.* Coward, McCann & Geoghegan, 1980.

10. B. S. Frey and A. Stutzer. "Happiness Prospers in Democracy." *Journal of Happiness Studies,* Vol. 1, No. 1, 2000, pp. 79–102.

Chapter 3

1. Frank Lloyd Wright. "America's Tomorrow." *American Architect,* May 1932, p. 32.

2. Earnest Elmo Calkins. "Beauty: The New Business Tool." *Atlantic Monthly,* August 1927, p. 152.

3. Stuart Ewen. *All Consuming Images: The Politics of Style in Contemporary Culture.* revised edition, Basic Books, 1999, p. 121.

Chapter 4

1. Eric Freyfogle. *Why Conservation Is Failing and How It Can Regain Ground.* Yale University Press, 2006.

2. World Commission on Environment and Development. "Our Common

Future." 1987. are.admin.ch/are/en/nachhaltig/international_uno/un terseite02330/ (Cited December 11, 2006)

3. Albert A. Bartlett. "Reflections on Sustainability, Population Growth, and the Environment—Revisited." *Renewable Resources Journal,* Vol. 15, No. 4, Winter 1997-1998, 6-23. hubbertpeak.com/bartlett/reflections .htm (Cited June 12, 2007)

4. Website: naturalstep.org

5. William E. Rees and Mathis Wackernagel. *Our Ecological Footprint.* New Society Publishers, 1995. Website: footprintnetwork.org

6. Bartlett 1998, op. cit.

7. Simon Dresner. *Principles of Sustainability.* Earthscan, 2002.
    Andres Edwards. *The Sustainability Revolution: Portrait of a Paradigm Shift.* New Society Publishers, 2005.

8. Jared Diamond. *Collapse: How Societies Choose to Fail or Succeed.* Viking, 2005.
    Joseph Tainter. *The Collapse of Complex Societies.* Cambridge University Press, 1988.

9. Julian Simon. "The State of Humanity: Steadily Improving." *Cato Policy Report,* Vol. 17, No. 5, p. 131.

10. Bartlett 1998, op. cit.

11. Simone Valente. "Sustainable Development, Renewable Resources and Technological Progress." *Environmental and Resource Economics,* Vol. 30, No. 1, January 2005, pp. 115–125.

12. Albert A. Bartlett. "Sustained Availability: A Management Program for Nonrenewable Resources." *American Journal of Physics,* Vol. 54, May 1986, pp. 398–402.

13. Richard Heinberg. *The Oil Depletion Protocol: A Plan to Avert Oil Wars, Terrorism and Economic Collapse.* New Society Publishers, 2006. Website: oildepletionprotocol.org

14. Marshall Sahlins. *Stone Age Economics.* Aldine, 1972.
    Gerhard Lenski. *Power and Privilege.* University of North Carolina Press, 1977.
    Ivan Illich. *Energy and Equity.* Calder and Boyars, 1974.

Chapter 5

1. Mark Bittner. *The Wild Parrots of Telegraph Hill.* Harmony Books, 2004. Mark Bittner's website is markbittner.net
    The Wild Parrots of Telegraph Hill. DVD. Directed by Judy Irving. pelicanmedia.org. All quotes are from the book.

2. Gary Snyder. *The Real Work: Interviews and Talks, 1964–1979.* New Directions, 1980.

3. Raymond C. Kelly. *Warless Societies and the Origin of War.* University of Michigan Press, 2000, pp. 20–21.

4. Max Weber. *The Vocation Lectures: "Science As a Vocation"; "Politics As a*

Vocation," ed. David Owen and Tracy B. Strong. Hackett Publishing Company, 2004.

5. Irene Pepperberg. *The Alex Studies: Cognitive and Communicative Abilities of Grey Parrots.* Harvard University Press, 2002.

6. Dinitia Smith. "A Thinking Bird, or Just Another Birdbrain?" *New York Times,* October 9, 1999.

Chapter 6

1. cepa.newschool.edu/het/profiles/malthus.htm (Cited December 11, 2006)

2. William Stanton. *The Rapid Growth of Human Populations 1750–2000.* Multi-Science Publishing, 2003, pp. 73–74.

3. peakoil.ie/newsletters/588 (Cited December 11, 2006)

4. Albert Bartlett. *Arithmetic, Population, and Energy.* DVD, University of Colorado, 2002.

Chapter 7

1. Lewis Aptekar. *Environmental Disasters in Global Perspective.* G. K. Hall, 1994, p. 110.

2. Samuel Prince. *Catastrophe and Social Change.* Columbia University Press, 1920.

3. Max Weber. *Economy and Society: An Outline of Interpretive Sociology.* Bedminster Press, 1968.

4. Benjamin McLuckie. *Italy, Japan, and the United States: Effects of Centralization on Disaster Responses 1964–1969.* Disaster Research Center, Ohio State University, 1977.

5. Lisa Rayner. *Ecological Collapse, Trauma Theory and Permaculture.* ecopsychology.org/journal/ezine/archive2/ecological_collapse.html (Cited June 12, 2007)

6. Rob Hopkins. *Is Our Collective Oil Dependence an Addiction?* energy bulletin.net/16846.html (Cited June 11, 2007)

7. World Health Organization. *Lexicon of Alcohol and Drug Terms.* who.int/substance_abuse/terminology/who_lexicon/en/ (Cited June 12, 2007)

8. Doug McKenzie-Mohr and William Smith. *Fostering Sustainable Behavior.* New Society Publishers, 1999.

Chapter 8

1. Energy Watch Group. *Coal: Resources and Future Production.* energy watchgroup.org/files/Coalreport.pdf (cited June 11, 2007)

2. David Fleming. *The Lean Guide to Nuclear Energy: A Life-Cycle in Trouble.* The Lean Economy Connection, 2006.

   See also: Energy Watch Group. *Uranium Resources and Nuclear Energy.* energiekrise.de/news/docs/specials2006/REO-Uranium_5-12-2006.pdf (Cited June 12, 2007)

Index

A

adaptation, 44

advertising, 40, 73, 137–138, 139, 162, 164

agriculture: after techno-collapse, 181, 182; Cuba's Special Period, 56–58; and environmental damage, 53, 54, 182; factors leading to famine, 48–50; genetic engineering of new crops, 54, 182; intensification through history, 35, 51–52; level of land cultivation, 12, 13; and numbers of farmers, 22, 49, 60–63; and Peak Oil, 22; plan for de-industrialization, 55, 59–63; in pre-history, 35, 47, 50–52; in US, 52–53, 57, 58, 61–63; and use of fossil fuels, 35, 48–49, 61, 116; world grain production, 10

airplanes, 72

All Consuming Images: On the Politics of Style in Contemporary Culture (Ewen), 74

alternative energy sources: in agriculture, 48–49; as savior after Peak Oil, 44, 79, 137, 175; as substitutes for non-renewable resources, 137, 153–154

Aptekar, Lewis, 131–132, 133

architecture, 68–69, 70–71

Art Deco, 73, 75

Art Nouveau, 70

arts, preservation of, 45–46, 63, 64, 79–81

Arts and Crafts movement, 67–72

Ashbee, C. R., 69

Asimov, Isaac, 120–121

B

Baby Boom generation: defining

moments, 165–166; development, 161, 162–164; disillusionment, 164–165; future, 172; politics, 169–171; wastefulness, 159

banking, 166

Bartlett, Albert A., 87, 90, 92, 119–120

Behrens, Peter, 73

Bellamy, Edward, 26

Bernays, Edward, 138, 139

biofuels, 48–49, 153–154

biointensive farming, 59–60, 63

Bittner, Mark, 97–100, 105–106, 110

Blood and Oil (Klare), 21

boom-and-bust cycles, 193

brain, development of, 187–188, 195

Braudel, Fernand, 201n1

Brokaw, Tom, 159, 160, 161

Brundtland Report, 86

Burne-Jones, Edward, 69

Bush, George H.W., 169

Bush, George W., 135, 171

business economics, 40, 90, 193

C

Calkins, E. E., 72

Campbell, C. J., 93, 118

Campbell, Joseph, 189

carbon dioxide emissions, 5. *see also* greenhouse gas emissions

carbon trading, 154–155

Carlowitz, Hanns Carl von, 86

cars, 72, 75

Carter, Jimmy, 169, 196

"Century of Self" (Curtis), 194

China, 154

CIA (Central Intelligence Agency), 137

cities, 75

civilization (*see also* industrializa-

tion): basis of, 109–110; development, 103–105; and emergent phenomena, 186–187; garbage from,
177–178; v. wild societies, 102–103,
105–106
climate, 5, 6, 50
Climate Change (*see also* psychology
of peak oil/climate change;
techno-collapse): after techno-
collapse, 181; benefits of cooperation with Peak Oil, 156–157; from
burning fossil fuels, 94, 152–153
(*see also* greenhouse gas emissions); concerted campaign for,
197; conflict with Peak Oil, 142–
143, 144–146; consequences of,
20–21, 50, 141, 145; experts in,
142, 143–144; peak levels of, 14–
15; possible strategies for, 148, 151–
153, 155–156; psychological theories
on, 127–135; scientific agreement
on, 18; strategies for psychologically coping with, 135–140
Clinton, Bill, 170
coal: "clean," 150, 151; future role,
149–151; and greenhouse gases,
94, 146, 147, 150–151; production
levels, 3, 153
Cold War, 168
The Collapse of Complex Societies
(Tainter), 89
Colodzin, Benjamin, 134
community building, 16, 63
computers, 37
conures, 107–108
Cornwall, England, 24
corporations, 55, 73–74, 166–167, 176
Crane, Walter, 69
CTL (coal-to-liquids), 150
Cuba's Special Period, 56–58, 59, 61
culture, preservation of, 45, 64, 65.
see also arts, preservation of
currency collapse, 176–177
Curtis, Adam, 194

D
Damasio, Antonio, 195–196

democracy, 18, 39, 64, 121
design: industrial, 72–75; and industrialized society, 67–71; in a
techno-collapsed world, 79–81
developing countries, 154
Diamond, Jared, 89
Diamond, Stanley, 41
dignity, 120–121

E
Earth Day, 167–168
economic inequality, 8, 13–14, 51–52,
95
economics: after techno-collapse,
176–177, 183; free market, 40, 90,
193; of future agriculture, 62–63;
and idea of steady growth, 119–
120, 193; and industrial revolution,
40, 193
education, 39, 62
egalitarianism, 95
Ehrlich, Paul, 128
emergent phenomena, 185–186
energy, 7–8, 163, 174. *see also* alternative energy sources; fossil fuels;
non–renewable resources
Energy and Equity (Illich), 8
environmental damage (*see also*
Climate Change): after techno-
collapse, 181–182; from agriculture, 53, 54, 182; by invasive
species, 108; and language barrier,
192–193
environmental movement, 167–168
EROEI (energy returned on energy
invested), 151, 154, 175
ethanol, 49
Ewen, Stuart, 74, 194
ExxonMobil, 148

F
famine: in early history, 47, 163,
201n1; prediction of, 48–50, 116
feedback loops, reinforcing, 7, 14,
51, 73, 144
fish harvests, 6, 11, 91–92
food production (*see also* agricul-

ture): after techno-collapse, 182; as key to human society, 38; and Malthus, 115–116; in pre-history, 47; and rationing, 62–63; in US, 47–48, 163; and use of fossil fuels, 48–49

forests, 91

fossil fuels (*see also* coal; natural gas; oil; tar sands): and agriculture, 35, 48–49, 61, 116; and concentrations of greenhouse gases, 5, 20, 93–95, 146, 147 (*see also* greenhouse gas emissions); consequences of continuing use of, 19–20, 92–93; earliest technology run on, 34–35, 193; and feedback loops, 7, 20; future of, 148–151; and hippie aesthetic, 77–78; and industrial revolution, 39, 163; and level of happiness, 16, 163–164; modern problems connected to, 21–22, 23–24; and modern technology, 36–37, 116, 174, 175; predictions on how long they will last, 3–4, 12, 145–148; scenarios of running out of, 55–56, 117–118; strategies for dealing with depletion of, 151–153; substitutes for, 153–154

Fostering Sustainable Behavior (MacKenzie-Mohr and Smith), 138–139

France, 201n1

Frank, Justin, 171

Freud, Sigmund, 137, 196

G

Gage, Phineas, 195

GDP (Gross Domestic Product), 17–18

generation gap, 164–165, 178–179

genetic engineering, 167, 182

genetically modified crops, 54, 182

Genuine Progress Indicator (GPI), 17

Gini index, 13–14

Glendinning, Chellis, 134

global warming, 14, 20, 144–145. *see also* Climate Change

Gore, Al, 145, 197

government: after techno-collapse, 45, 121, 180–181; and beginnings of political organization, 104; and democracy, 18, 39, 64, 121; environmental legislation, 167–168; and language, 195; reaction to disaster, 132, 140; reaction to Peak Oil, 140, 197; and sustainability measures, 95–96

GPI (Genuine Progress Indicator), 18

grain, 10

Great Britain, 147–148

The Greatest Generation (Brokaw), 159, 160, 161

greenhouse gas emissions: from coal, 94, 146, 147, 150–151; concentrations by source, 146, 147; from fossil fuels, 5, 20, 93–95, 146, 147; how much they need to be reduced, 152–153; peak levels, 14; strategies for reducing, 152–155

Gross Domestic Product (GDP), 17–18

growth v. sustainability, 18, 42, 119–120, 174, 194, 196

H

Haber-Bosch process, 52

Hansen, James, 146, 147

happiness, 15–16

Harris, Marvin, 38

Hawkins, Louis W., 69

Heather, Peter, 133

heavy oil, 151

Herman, Judith, 134

hippies, 77–78, 164, 165, 166

Hirsch, Robert, 140

Holmgren, David, 59

Hopkins, Rob, 135–136, 140

horticulture, 63

Hubbard, Elbert, 70–71

Hubbert, M. King, 147, 166

Huebner, Jonathan, 42–44

human rights, 120–121
Human Scale (Sale), 64
hydrocarbons. *see* fossil fuels

I

ideological changes: away from fossil
    fuels, 23–24; away from industrial-
    ization, 63–65; from perpetual
    growth to sustainability, 18, 42,
    119–120, 174, 193, 196; role of
    language in, 196
Illich, Ivan, 8
An Inconvenient Truth (Gore), 145,
    197
Indian Line Farm, 62
industrial design, 72–75, 75–76
industrialization (*see also* fossil fuels;
    techno-collapse): adapted to dis-
    asters, 133; and crafts, 67–68; his-
    tory of, 31–37, 116, 193; how it's
    changed humans, 31–32, 37–39,
    109–110, 174, 175; and industrial
    revolution, 39–40, 163, 193; mod-
    ern criticism of, 31–33, 41–42; plan
    for de-industrialization, 55, 59–63;
    as savior, 44, 175; weeding our-
    selves off, 63–65
inventions, 42–44
Iroquois, 46, 86
Irving, Judy, 97, 99

J

Jackson, Wes, 59
Jeavons, John, 59–60

K

Kelly, R. C., 102
Klare, Michael, 21
Kübler-Ross, Elisabeth, 128–129, 130

L

labor, 15–16, 35
Lahontan, Baron de, 101
The Land Institute, 59
land use, 13, 62
language: and belief in symbols, 189;
    development, 186–187, 195; and

economics, 193; and environmen-
    tal damage, 192–193; and politics,
    194; and reason, 190–192; and re-
    ligion, 187–190; role in civilization,
    109, 186; and societal change, 27,
    196, 197–198
leisure time, 15–16
Lerro, Bruce, 189
lifestyle choices, 15–16, 16–17
The Limits to Growth (Club of
    Rome), 168
local economies, 22, 55
logic, 190–193, 195
Looking Backward: 2000–1887 (Bel-
    lamy), 26
love, 110

M

MacKenzie-Mohr, Doug, 139
Macy, Joanna, 129–130
magical thinking, 191, 192, 193
Malthus, Thomas, 114–117
Mandil, Claude, 199n1
marketing, 137–140. *see also* advertis-
    ing
McLuckie, Benjamin, 133
media, 45, 162, 182–183
Mexico, 16
Millennium Ecosystem Assessment,
    18
Mollison, Bill, 59
money trading, 176
morality, 120–121, 189–190
Morris, William, 67–69
Moyers, Bill, 120
Müller, Max, 189
Mumford, Lewis, 32, 33
The Myth of the Machine (Mumford),
    33
mythology, 189–190

N

natural gas, 2, 3, 148–149, 153
The Natural Step, 86–87
nature, 103–105
Nelson, Gaylord, 167
Nixon, Richard, 169

non-renewable resources, 92–95. *see also* fossil fuels
nuclear power, 154

O

oil (*see also* Peak Oil): as bulwark of US economy, 166–167; level of dependency on, 135–136, 137; production levels, 2, 151, 153; substitutes for, 90; sustainability, 92–93; and wars, 22
Oil Depletion Protocol, 93
oil shale, 151
Oman, 148
Ornstein, Robert, 128

P

parrots, 98–101, 105–108, 110
Pauli, Wolfgang, 191
Peak Oil (*see also* psychology of peak oil/climate change; techno-collapse): benefits of cooperation with Climate Change, 156–157; concerted campaign for, 197; conflict with Climate Change, 142–143, 144–146; definition, 1; depletionists' and their views, 144–145, 149–151, 153; effects of, 141, 145; experts in, 141–142, 143; possible strategies for, 151–152, 153–155, 155–156; predictions of when it will happen, 145–148; psychological theories on, 127–135; strategies for psychologically coping with, 135–140; in US, 166
Pepperberg, Irene, 106–107
permaculture, 59, 63, 78, 79
petrochemicals, 94
politics (*see also* government): after techno-collapse, 180–181; beginnings of political organization, 104; in a de-industrialized society, 64–65; and greenhouse gas emissions, 155–156; and the industrial revolution, 39–40; and population explosion, 121–122; and quasi-religious ideologies, 194;

role in changing society, 196–197; and success of technology, 41–42; and sustainability measures, 95–96; in US, 169–172
pollution, 21, 93–95
Poon, Wing-Chi, 143
population: and A. Bartlett, 119–120; and I. Asimov, 120–121; level through history, 11; methods of controlling, 119, 121, 122–123, 190; and politics, 121–122; and sustainability, 90–91; and T. Malthus, 115–116; and W. Stanton, 117–118
post-traumatic stress disorder (PTSD), 130–135
poverty, 12–13, 116, 154–155. *see also* economic inequality
Prince, Samuel, 132
progress as an idea, 18, 193, 196
psychological maturity, 128
psychology of peak oil/climate change: described as addiction and dependency, 135–137; and mass behavior change, 138–140, 196–197; and post-traumatic stress disorder, 130–135; and response to crisis, 23–24, 127–128; treated like grief, 128–130

R

The Rapid Growth of Human Populations, 1750-2000 (Stanton), 117
Rayner, Lisa, 134
Reagan, Ronald, 169
The Real Work (Snyder), 97–98
Rees, William, 87
religion: after techno-collapse, 183; development, 187–191, 192; in politics, 194
renewable resources, 91–92, 94, 153–154. *see also* alternative energy sources
Robèrt, Karl-Henrik, 86
Rockefeller, John D., 166–167
Rolfe, Douglas, 41
Roosevelt, Eleanor, 58
Roycrofters, 70, 71

Ruskin, John, 68–69
Russia (Soviet Union), 168

S

Sale, Kirkpatrick, 64
Sasol, 150
Saving Private Ryan, 161
science, preservation of, 45
scientific method, development of,
    192
September 11th, 2001, 171
sequestration, 95, 147, 150, 151
Smith, William, 139
Snyder, Gary, 97, 109
social marketing, 137–140
social welfare, 7–8, 117
societal change (*see also* ideological
    changes; techno-collapse): and
    language, 27, 196–197, 198; and
    politics, 64–65, 197
solar power, 175
Soviet Union, 168
specialization, 35, 51–52, 104–105
species extinction, 181
spirituality, 183. *see also* religion
Stanton, William, 117–118, 121, 122
starlings, 107
Stephenson, George, 40
Strauss, Leo, 194
sustainability: axioms of, 88–95; defi-
    nition of, 85; history of concept,
    86–88; and politics, 95–96; v.
    growth, 18, 42, 119–120, 174, 194,
    196
symbolism, 189, 194

T

Tainter, Joseph, 88–89
tar sands, 90, 151
techno-collapse: aesthetic of, 79–81;
    anger and violence during, 178–
    180; and communications, 179,
    182–183; description of, 175–177,
    178; and environment, 181–182;
    and government, 45, 121, 180–181;
    J. Tainter's view of, 89; and poli-
tics, 180–181; severity of, 20–21,
    44–45, 182; suggestions for sur-
    vival, 45–46, 183
technology. *see* industrialization;
    techno-collapse
Terkel, Studs, 161

U

United States: agriculture, 52–53, 57,
    58, 61–63; Baby Boom generation,
    159, 162–164; energy production,
    149, 163–164; environmental
    movement, 167–168; food pro-
    duction, 47–48, 163; and Gross
    Domestic Product, 17; hours
    spent on the job in, 15–16; oil as
    bulwark of economy, 166–167;
    politics, 169–172
uranium, 4, 6, 175
Urinetown, 25, 113–114

V

Victory Gardens, 57, 58
Vietnam War, 165
violence, 179–180. *see also* war

W

war: after techno-collapse, 180; in
    civilized society, 102; and connec-
    tion to fossil fuels, 21–22, 145;
    Vietnam, 165; World War II, 161–
    162
water: after techno-collapse, 181–182;
    arctic ice melt, 144; consumption
    levels, 9–10, 91; and glacier re-
    treat, 143; scarcity of fresh, 49–50
Weber, Max, 132–133
The Wild Parrots of Telegraph Hill
    (Bittner), 25, 97–101, 105–108,
    110
women, 40–41, 51
World War II, 161–162
Wright, Frank Lloyd, 70, 71

Z

Zerzan, John, 32, 41–42, 45

About the Author

RICHARD HEINBERG is the author of seven previous books including *The Party's Over: Oil, War and the Fate of Industrial Societies* (New Society, 2003, 2005), *Powerdown: Options and Actions for a Post-Carbon World* (New Society, 2004), and *The Oil Depletion Protocol* (New Society, 2006). He is an educator, editor, lecturer, a Core Faculty member of New College of California's Campus for Sustainable Living, and a Fellow of the Post Carbon Institute. He is widely regarded as one of the world's foremost Peak Oil educators.

He has also authored scores of essays and articles, which have appeared in journals such as *The American Prospect, Quarterly Review, Public Policy Research, Resurgence, The Futurist, European Business Review, Earth Island Journal;* and on web sites such as *GlobalPublicMedia.com, Alternet.org, EnergyBulletin.net, ProjectCensored.com,* and *Counterpunch.com.*

In 2005, *Powerdown* received *ForeWord* magazine's Bronze Environmental Award. In 2007, *The Oil Depletion Protocol* won *ForeWord's* Gold Environmental Award as well as the Independent Publishers Book of the Year (IPPY) Bronze Award in the category of Current Events.

His books have been translated into eight languages.

Since 2002, he has given over three hundred lectures on oil depletion ("Peak Oil") to a wide variety of audiences, including members of the European Parliament.

He is the recipient of the M. King Hubbert Award for Excellence in Energy Education (2006).

Heinberg appears prominently in the documentary films *11th Hour* (produced and narrated by Leonardo diCaprio, 2007); *Asleep in America* (2007); The History Channel's *Megadisasters* series, episode on Peak Oil (2007); *What a Way to Go: Life at the End of Empire* (2007); *Escape from Suburbia* (2007); *Crude Impact* (2006); the nationally televised PBS documentary *Ripe for Change* (2006); *The Power of Community: How Cuba Survived Peak Oil* (2006); and *The End of Suburbia* (2004). He is currently working with Discovery Channel on the upcoming sustainability series, *Final Hour.*

For more information on Richard and his current work,
go to www.richardheinberg.com

If you have enjoyed *Peak Everything*, you might also enjoy other

BOOKS TO BUILD A NEW SOCIETY

Our books provide positive solutions for people who want to
make a difference. We specialize in:

Sustainable Living • Ecological Design and Planning
Natural Building & Appropriate Technology
Environment and Justice • Conscientious Commerce
Progressive Leadership • Resistance and Community • Nonviolence
Educational and Parenting Resources

New Society Publishers

ENVIRONMENTAL BENEFITS STATEMENT

New Society Publishers has chosen to produce this book on recycled paper made
with 100% post consumer waste, processed chlorine free, and old growth free.

For every 5,000 books printed, New Society saves the following resources:[1]

33	Trees
3,028	Pounds of Solid Waste
3,331	Gallons of Water
4,345	Kilowatt Hours of Electricity
5,504	Pounds of Greenhouse Gases
24	Pounds of HAPs, VOCs, and AOX Combined
8	Cubic Yards of Landfill Space

[1]Environmental benefits are calculated based on research done by the Environmental Defense
Fund and other members of the Paper Task Force who study the environmental impacts of the
paper industry.

For a full list of NSP's titles, please call 1-800-567-6772 *or check out our web site at:*

www.newsociety.com

NEW SOCIETY PUBLISHERS